Lust for Life

Lust for Life

Tales of Sex & Love

Edited by Claude Lalumière & Elise Moser

Véhicule Press

Published with the generous assistance of The Canada Council for
the Arts, the Book Publishing Industry Development Program of the
Department of Canadian Heritage and the Société de développement des
entreprises culturelles du Québec (SODEC).

Cover design: J.W. Stewart
Set in Adobe Minion by Simon Garamond
Printed by Marquis Book Printing Inc.

LIBRARY AND ARCHIVES CANADA CATALOGUING IN PUBLICATION

Lust for Life : tales of sex and love /
Claude Lalumière and Elise Moser, editors

ISBN 1-55065-203-6

1. Erotic stories, Canadian (English). 2. Erotic stories, American.
3. Love stories, Canadian (English). 4. Love stories, American.
5. Canadiar fiction (English)—21st century. 6. American fiction—21st
century. I. Lalumière, Claude II. Moser, Elise

PS8323.E75L87 2006   C813'.01083538   C2005-907136-2

Published by Véhicule Press, Montréal, Québec, Canada
www.vehiculepress.com

Distribution in Canada by LitDistCo
orders@litdistco.ca

Distribution in U.S. by Independent Publishers Group
www.ipgbook.com

Printed on 100% post-consumer recycled paper

Printed and bound in Canada

Contents

Introduction

Sex and love are experiences enhanced by being shared. Similarly, this anthology of fiction about sex and love required a communion of ideas, tastes, and perspectives—a mingling of creative juices. And so a project that began as one editor's passion has fulfilled its promise in the conjoined efforts of two co-editors and twenty-three authors.

More than five hundred writers responded to our call for "smart, literate, witty, moving, challenging fiction that explores desire, gender, sexuality, taboos, and the human body with insight and without inhibitions." We read stories from all over the world, tales that showcased a wide range of sexual experiences, romantic entanglements, and literary styles and genres.

From this cornucopia of possibilities, we selected a wealth of exceptional tales. The stories in this book made us laugh or cry, shocked or amused us, excited or disturbed us—or, often, made us feel several of those emotions at once. Each of these stories captures—in its own unique and unforgettable way—the essence of the anthology's title: that our constant yearning for sex, love, pleasure, and each other is, most profoundly, a lust for life.

MATTHEW ANDERSON

Charity in Her Flesh

Virgil runs his finger between the plastic tab in his clerical shirt and the dampness of his Adam's apple. He teases the opening back and forth, a reflex in the heat. From his vantage near the sacristy he watches two men in their fifties, the fathers of the bride and groom, shift uncomfortably as they stand at the back of the church. In turn and almost by instinct, they wipe their brows, put their hands on each others' shoulders and smile mirthlessly at exclamations of humour he cannot hear. This is a ritual, Virgil understands. It is meant to reassure each man that the contract is still on. Standing to one side, the groom is mute. He knows. Virgil also knows.

The property is not cooperating.

"There are times in life when plans..." Virgil practices the phrase to the corner of the carpet, *sotto voce*. No, he decides: too wishy-washy. *Don't apologize.* "Although it can seem a shock, love sometimes requires..." Requires is a good word.

Looking at the frayed end of carpet there comes to Virgil's mind a memory of lace. As a young child, he had always imagined its softness. But at his first tentative adolescent explorations of a girl's breasts his fingers were shocked by the stiff roughness of the edging of the fabric, the almost accusatory way it had poked back.

Virgil spies the sexton reading behind the baptistery and sends him out to open the doors in the hope of catching a breeze. He wonders if he should remove his rector's alb, but at this point the shirt beneath is soaked through. Outside, what was a torrential downpour is speedily evaporating off the sidewalk. The sun's breakthrough in the last few minutes has sharply increased the temperature in the nave. Condensation covers the side of Virgil's glass, leaving rings on the table. There will be hell to pay with the parish ladies if he doesn't find a coaster soon, but who thinks of coasters for a church?

While he is considering this, the organist, on her second run through

9

her entire repertoire, simply stops mid-piece. Being paid a flat rate, and never one for improvisation (a qualification proudly announced to Virgil on a number of occasions), she slouches, arms sullenly crossed, at the console.

Curious guests, surprised at the sudden quiet, swivel in the pews to peer at the back. Mr. Languay, father of the bride, keeps clearing his throat, a high-pitched choking sound and the only noise to break the silence left by the disgruntled organist. His square butcher's face, always ruddy, is now very nearly purple. Virgil scans the pews again and notes the rigid posture of those among the invited who have not yet given up decorum to turn and stare, despite the obvious breakdown of the music. These will be the last to forgive.

People have already been kept waiting thirty minutes. Ten minutes ago, Virgil made an announcement that there would be a delay. This was true, but disingenuous. Virgil made it sound as if he knew the reason, as if it were a simple matter of logistics—say, parking the limousine—when in fact he knew that the bride was already in the building. He begins to feel a pressure building in his head. Unless he makes another announcement—or does something at least—they may begin to leave.

He walks to his study, knocks, and steps quickly in. A woman is in the chair—his chair. She is covered, carelessly, in a towel. Her bare feet are propped on his daytimer, her hands flapping, another woman standing over her with bobby pins in her mouth. He realizes the office door is still open behind him. He closes it quickly. A naked woman.

"Oh God oh God, I don't know if I can do this. Allison, take this brush. Jesus Christ—oops, sorry, Virgil."

"It's okay." He is finding it hard to take a full breath.

"No—"

"No, it's okay." If he had a penny for every time someone had apologized for swearing in his presence...

"Jesus, I've got the jitters."

"It's fine. Just fine. You've got lots of time." Virgil lies. He feels a sense of foreboding.

"Really?"

"Really. There's nothing else booked for today except you." Virgil opens his hands wide on "you," the same gesture he uses at communion.

"I can't, you know, think like this. It's too much pressure. I don't know how the hell I wound up here."

Not being eager to give an opinion, Virgil makes a slight movement with his lips. He lifts his shoulders a second, then drops them.

Her name is Chase. Chase for Charity, she told Virgil. She had printed *Charity* on the official form, slowly, as if reluctant to admit to it. Virgil had liked her immediately. Although she would never know it, his first view of Chase—from the back, as she bent over to remove a sandal while he rounded the corner from the sacristy—had much to do with his fascination. Unseen, he had been overwhelmed by the simple sensuality of that act and by the incongruity of his own reaction in this austere and familiar space. He had noticed then the small but rather ornate Celtic cross tattooed on the skin of the small of her back. When, later, the subject of tattoos came up, their conversation moved naturally from her skin to his religion, a change of topic that brought Virgil equal parts relief and disappointment.

Chase, the child of hippie parents, had moved "back" east from Salt Spring Island, mimicking the rebellion that had taken her parents to the west coast in the first place. She had landed a job in the city's burgeoning film industry, working her way up to her most recent stint as second assistant director on a Sunday night TV drama titled *Eyes of a Terrorist.*

"Promise me you'll watch it," she had said to Virgil, "I really want to know what you think." He had told her that his television only gets two channels, but she did not remember. After the third meeting, Chase informed Virgil that he already knew more about her than any other man, more even than her fiancé. Virgil finds himself remembering these words when he turns off the light in his kitchen at night.

Chase met the groom at a resort in the Dominican Republic during a dance that involved passing a cocktail glass beneath layers of clothing. They have been living together for two years. "She's a wild thing," the groom said once to Virgil, a passing comment, perhaps a confession. "And I'm the settling-down type."

Chase's towel has slipped enough so that, if he were to move slightly closer, one of her nipples would be visible. Virgil stays by the door.

"What do you think all those people out there would do if I didn't go through with it?"

Virgil keeps his voice steady. "They'd live." He pauses. He thinks about truth, and weddings. About Mr. Languay. "Okay. Some would be upset."

"My God, some? The flowers alone cost five hundred bucks." Allison gives Chase a cigarette. Chase lights it as Virgil watches. She takes a long drag, then breathes it out against the bookcase. His bookcase. There are no ashtrays anywhere in the building.

"People would get over it eventually. I didn't know you smoked."

"I don't." Her eyes focus on him finally, in a way that now makes him feel uncomfortable. "So you think I shouldn't go through with it?"

"That's not what I'm saying."

'Then what are you saying?"

"I'm just saying..." he notices a hint of a whine in his voice. Where did that come from? "I'm saying ... Listen: you have to be true to, to—your fears, sure. But also to what brought you here."

She snorts, interrupting him. "Do you have any idea how much we've spent?"

"That's not the point. The big issues haven't changed, have they? Does he know the person he's marrying?"

"I think so." She looks out his window. He watches the way her face is profiled against the light, the languor of her outstretched arm, the way the towel falls away from her leg. The pose is one he will shake his head to clear, later, sitting in that chair, working on his sermons. "I believe so."

"Do you know who you are marrying?"

She looks back at him. "I think so."

"Then?"

There is a silence. "Then." Chase's shoulders settle. "Okay." She repeats herself: "Okay." Virgil turns quickly as she begins to stand. He hears the towel fall onto the carpet—and steps out.

Ten minutes later, Virgil is standing with a much-relieved groom at the front of the church. The organist plays "Ave Maria." An unbearable humidity has settled here in the altar area, where there are no windows. The sound of a siren wails past the building, momentarily rising like a troubled aria from the salutation of the blessed Virgin.

Virgil does not know the bridesmaid, who flew in only last night from Vancouver. But clearly she has done this before. She walks the length of the chancel slowly, as if it were a runway. She smiles broadly for the photographer and takes her appointed place to the left of the altar. On cue the bride moves into view at the back of the church holding Mr. Languay's arm; without announcement the gathered friends and family stand.

It used to be that it was only at the altar that men were granted their first view of the child-brides arranged for them and adorned for their pleasure. Chase, in unconscious imitation of this custom, has insisted that the groom not see her in her dress until now.

She told Virgil she found it in a specialized used-clothing shop near the market area, spending far more than the already rich purchase price to have side and back buttons added to the open-shouldered bodice so it would fit her wider chest. The satin had required extensive work also, to repair, blanch, and in some places replace the inevitable yellowing of the years. What some couples pay for a small reception Chase had laid out to create just the right cream shimmer that makes her now seem to flow, rather than step, up the aisle.

Virgil is lost in the sight. It is in the peculiar alchemy of a wedding, he thinks, that, no matter what, the entrance of the bride always seems to work magic. Chase is wearing small white flowers in a crown that weaves in and out of her hair. The tight material on her torso is drawn into a V-shape, from where it cascades outward and back. The same flowers as are in her hair strew the train so that she appears to be one of Shakespeare's faery princesses arising from a medieval forest glade to meet her love.

Virgil glances at the frescoes around him in the altar, where men and women with the faces of hard-working peasants, likely the family of the German artist who originally did the paintings, peer down piously on the procession. Higher yet, the stained-glass apostles baking in the sun above stare straight ahead, august in their androgyny.

About halfway to the front there is a slight but audible sound, a *pip* that makes Virgil momentarily turn to the baptismal font to check if something is dripping. Seeing nothing, he turns again to watch Chase, who also seems momentarily distracted by the sound.

Again: *pip*. Virgil thinks of water, of the sound a child might make with spitballs, of fish mouths, of chewing gum, of things dropped. He scans the pews.

The groom looks at Chase and then, turning, at Virgil right beside him. Virgil keeps his smile open and as relaxed as possible, a basic response drilled into him by dozens of minor wedding pitfalls. Chase is moving forward more slowly, an uncertain look on her face. Virgil sees a carefully curled lock of Chase's hair fall, releasing one of the flowers.

Something shoots into a pew on the pulpit side, hits the floor, and rolls. Virgil strains forward to see what it is, as do dozens of others.

Pip. This time the object hits the train and falls straight down, gathering momentum until it rolls like a muffled penny into the middle of the aisle. It is, Virgil sees now, a satin-covered button. Chase half-turns to see what is happening to her dress. The act of turning seems to loosen the bodice of the outfit. Now, incongruously, Chase's bare shoulders and torso appear to rotate to her left while the dress itself, like a stubborn dance partner, remains pointed forward. Then another button snaps.

Father and daughter stop mid-step, halfway to the altar, a look of horror spreading over Chase's features, her fingertips white now on her father's arm. Her half-turn has broken the form of the bodice; released from its hold, its three pieces begin now to fall outward with growing speed, like the petals of an autumn flower. Chase grabs for the material, but it is too late. It slides off her breasts and collapses at her feet. Except for her shoes, Chase is naked.

If there is a gasp from the guests Virgil does not hear it. He is keeping his eyes firmly on Chase's, for at this moment she is looking directly at him, and he knows that anything else is betrayal.

For a moment there is absolute panic in her eyes. Virgil keeps looking at her, she at him. For how long—three seconds? five seconds?—they stand like that. Then she sighs and purses her lips. Then she steps out of the collapsed dress. She bends over, does something to her sandals and kicks them off as well. Virgil notices another tattoo.

Chase once more takes Mr. Languay's arm. Her father clears his throat, then does it again and again, like the sound of a small gas-starved motor that someone insists on trying to start.

The organist, who had complained to Virgil about the couple's choice of Gounod and who is likely wishing she had insisted on the more familiar Schubert version of "Ave Maria," finally seems to notice what has happened. Out of the corner of his eye Virgil sees her throw up her hands reflexively at the sight of a naked woman in the middle of the sanctuary. The action knocks the partition from the stand, hitting all the keys at once in a brief but glorious thunderclap of tones.

In the reverberating silence, Virgil watches Chase and her father move forward and arrive at the first pew, ending their procession exactly where they had practiced Friday evening. Mr. Languay is now weeping. The groom, as if in a trance, steps out and shakes hands with Mr. Languay.

Again, exactly as rehearsed. Everyone then stands unmoving.

They are all looking at Virgil. Outside the church a car passes, radio blaring. Virgil hears the words: "...don't let this night be over, no baby no never let it be done..." He looks down at the book in his hands. He sees, as if someone else had done it, where the text was marked for the ceremony. When in doubt, read, he thinks. Read *slowly*. "If I speak in the tongues of mortals and of angels," he begins, "but do not have love, I am a noisy gong or a clanging cymbal."

The groom startles at the words. Then he takes off his suit coat. He steps forward with it, protectively, to cover Chase's nakedness but then stops. He looks up and off to the side, as if considering whether or not it might rain.

Virgil, realizing that he has stopped reading, continues: "And if I understand all mysteries and all knowledge, and if I have all faith, so as to remove mountains, but do not have love, I am nothing."

The groom looks again at Virgil and at the altar with its flowers. He lets the jacket fall. He looks from Chase down to his feet. And then, very slowly, he bends over.

For a second Virgil thinks that the groom is about to throw up. But no: he begins to untie his shoes. He removes socks and pants. Then his shirt. When he pulls down his briefs there is a noise from the assembled group, as if everyone holding their breath had finally let it go.

"And if I give away all I possess to the poor and hand over my body so that I may boast but do not have love, I gain nothing."

Now that he is also naked, the groom stands almost shyly, as if out of further ideas. Chase kisses Mr. Languay and sits him down in the pew beside her mother, who is fanning herself. Chase takes the groom in tow. For the first time since Virgil has seen her today, she is beaming. The photographer, recovered, is snapping pictures without pause. The couple arrive before the altar.

"So then, these three remain: faith, hope, and love. But the greatest of these is love."

For a moment Virgil is lost in thought looking at them. He has the incredible feeling, as if they were his, of their feet and how it must feel to put bare flesh against the dark wood of the floor, the cool marble of the altar stairs.

The organist noisily climbs out of her organ bench, exiting through the sacristy door. Uncomprehending, Virgil turns to watch her back, like a driver watching his own car wreck in slow-motion progress. When he turns again to the altar, they are all looking at him. Everyone in the church.

"Just the shoes and socks," he announces. "I'm just taking off my shoes and socks."

Catherine Lundoff

Emily Says

Stacia can't see Emily, not even when she's lying between us at night with her fingers twisted up inside me. Not even when all I can feel is the warm pressure of her breasts against mine, her breath hot on my skin. She can't even see her when I come, when Emily's fingers and tongue pull my orgasms out of me and I jump around and moan right next to her. Stacia just goes on sleeping like she's in a coma or something while Emily laughs and laughs, licking my juices from her fingers.

It used to be Stacia's fingers inside me, her tongue in my mouth at night. I miss riding the sweaty length of her thigh, tonguing her nipples against my teeth. She doesn't disappear in the morning like Emily does. She doesn't leave me feeling exhausted and sick but so horny I don't know what I'm doing. She even used to love me. I think.

It didn't use to be like this before Emily came. I guess I was happy. But it's so hard to remember back that far, especially when Emily's around. It seems like forever even though I know that it can't have been that long. I think it's only been a month, maybe two. You know how it goes: one day you're in a relationship, bed death looming on the horizon, the next you've picked up a hot babe who takes over your life. I'm just lucky because only I can see her. At least I think that's true. Maybe Stacia's just ignoring her, waiting for the right time to dump me. I know that's what Emily would say. She says a lot of stuff like that, as long as I only want to talk about Stacia. It's a lot harder to get her to talk about herself.

Last week I asked her why Stacia couldn't see her, and she just smiled. It wasn't a happy smile, more like an *I've got a secret* smile. Then she rubbed herself against me, her thigh slick against my clit while she kissed me hard. I couldn't help myself: I kissed her back until I didn't have any more questions.

But they came back the next day when I was sitting at my desk trying not to fall asleep. At least I didn't have to call in sick. Lately I do that more and more. When Emily's not around, I can remember all the things I can't think of when she's there. Like I think I can remember meeting her at the bar. Or maybe it was at a party. I do remember that she came home with us and Stacia passed out and then it was just her and me. But Stacia can't remember any of that.

Emily says she loves me and that she'll be mine until the end. I keep meaning to ask what she means by that. I mean is it like "till death do us part" or what? Stacia said something like that once, back before she started falling asleep right after dinner, back before I started spending a few hours on the couch with Emily every night.

I don't know much about Emily except what she likes to do in bed. But I'm not like that, not really. Last week, I even tried to get her to watch TV with me. I thought maybe we could talk. Instead, she unzipped my jeans and tore a hole in my underwear with her long red nails. Nobody ever went down on me like Emily does. When she slipped her tongue inside me, swiping its rough edge against my clit, I was all hers. But then I guess I've been all hers since she first showed up.

My clit was on fire, and I could feel the couch getting soaked underneath me the minute she touched me. She even hummed a little while she worked her fingers up inside me, like a cat purring. It feels so good when she does me, better than any other girl, better than any sex toy you can imagine. It's like she can't get enough and neither can I. She licked and licked, each swipe of her tongue, every thrust of her fingers filling me, until I bucked and heaved against her mouth. Then she laughed when I tried to moan into the pillows so Stacia wouldn't hear.

"She won't hear a thing. I promise." Then she stood up and started stripping in front of the TV, slow and sure like a pro. Once she was naked, she sat on my lap, wrapping her long legs around my waist. I was panting when she kissed me, groaning into her gorgeous breasts when she yanked my shirt and bra off. She arched her back as I worked my hand between her legs and thrust my fingers inside her. She came, or at least I think she did. Then she pulled my hand out of her and sucked on my fingers until I ached so bad that she went down on me again.

Sometimes I worry that she's not getting anything out of this, or even that she's faking it. She makes all the right noises, tastes the way she should, even smells like it's real, but I still have my doubts. But she's so beautiful, so perfect, that even her missing belly button doesn't freak me out anymore. It did at first. I mean, I'm not stupid. I know she's not like other girls I've been with. No zits, no wrinkles, not even a mole or a wart, and she wants sex all the time. That's kind of weird, right?

I used to dream about having someone like this. Now I don't dream at all, or, if I do, I only dream about Emily. I can see her, naked and perfect every time I close my eyes. I walk around smelling of sex, wet and hot for her all day. If I go into a bathroom, I dream about her taking me up against the wall, her strong fingers covering my mouth so no-one else can hear me. Sometimes, I lean against the tile walls of the bathroom at work, my fingers down my pants, rubbing and rubbing until I think my skin will come off. But I can't do it like Emily does.

I wonder what Stacia dreams about.

Emily says that Stacia's going to leave me. She's seen the signs before. First they lose interest in sex, then they lose interest in everything else. Stacia didn't even kiss me hello when I came home today. When I tried to kiss her, she said, "I'm too tired. Could you please just take a shower? How can any human being be this horny?" I hate it when she says stuff like that. I just want to be held and touched, feel someone's naked body against mine. Someone's fingers and tongue on my skin. Stacia's just trying to make me feel bad about my needs. That's what Emily says.

I need, I need, I need it all the time. And Emily gives it to me. She comes in when I'm in the shower, washing off the cloud of lust that hangs around me ever since I met her. That's the smell that Stacia can't stand now, but I can remember when she loved the way I smelled. Or at least she said she did. Emily says that she was lying. Now Emily's bright red lips are sucking on my nipple, and she's working one finger up my ass. I'm so empty that I ache whenever she's not inside me. I crave the feel of her skin against mine, the weight of her breasts in my hands. I'd die without her, I just know I would.

I tell her that, but she just smiles. The water is cascading down on us, and I'm caressing her, trying to reach down to cup her flawless ass in my desperate hands. My body is all hers now, and I shake in her arms until they're the only thing holding me on my feet. I don't bother trying to be quiet.

Then Stacia throws the door open and just stands there looking at me. I can hear Emily laughing, but I don't think Stacia can see her. She just looks at me and shakes her head and turns away. "Stacia! Come in here with us! C'mon, baby..." I stop when I see the look on her face.

"Us? There is no 'us,' sweetie, unless you've started giving your fingers or the showerhead their own names. You're freaking me out.

Finish up, and let's have dinner." She turns away again, and Emily sucks harder, her sharp little teeth sinking into my nipple until I yelp. But Stacia just closes the door and doesn't look back. Whatever Stacia dreams about, it isn't me. Emily's right. She doesn't love me anymore.

The thought makes me very sad for a moment. Then Emily's mouth is sucking on my clit and her finger thrusts into my ass and I don't think anymore. At least not about anything else. She works the fingers of her other hand up inside me, and I grab at the towel rack to keep from falling over. Her fingers make a fist, stretching me wide as I can go. Pussy and ass filled all at once, and her little sandpaper tongue on my clit until I come—shaking all over, knees giving out—and slide down the tiles into the tub.

Emily kisses my clit tenderly and runs a finger down my jaw, almost like Stacia used to. Then she kisses me, lets me lick my own taste from her mouth. And when she's done kissing me, she jumps out of the shower and walks out the door, no towel around her or anything. I start to yell after her to put something on until I remember that Stacia can't see her anyway. Unless Stacia's lying about that, too.

Emily stops in the hallway and smiles back at me with those red, red lips. Her eyes don't smile with her mouth though, and it makes her look hungry and fierce. I shiver a little, but the big empty space in my pussy where her fingers live is aching again, so much that I ignore the feeling and hold my arms out to her. She blows me an air kiss and disappears down the hall.

I wonder where she goes so that I can't see her either. Maybe she lives in a different dimension where there's another version of Stacia and me. I wipe the mist off the mirror and wonder what she sees in me. I'm not beautiful like her and most of the time I just look tired. Right now I think I look sick. The skin is hanging loose off my ribs and my breasts look smaller. There are huge circles under my eyes and my skin is kind of yellow. Not surprising since I never get any sleep anymore. But that's okay because Emily loves me anyway.

I get dressed, stumbling around in a fog. When I walk into the kitchen, Stacia's waiting for me; there's some other woman I've never seen sitting at the table with her. "This is Sam," she says, like this should mean something to me. "She just dropped by for dinner."

Sam stands up and holds her hand out for me to shake. She's got short grey hair and a calm smile. She shakes my hand just right, not too short and not too long, like she's had a lot of practice at it. That's when Emily comes in. It doesn't look like Sam can see her either. She leans over the back of my chair and whispers, "Stacia brought home a shrink. She thinks you're nuts." She laughs when I glare at Stacia.

Stacia knows how I feel about shrinks, knows what they did to me when I was a kid. Once I even told her about the electroshock they used to try and make me straight. How could she do this to me? I make a huge effort and shove Emily back as gently as I can. "I'm not crazy! Just because I want sex once in a while doesn't mean that I've got a problem! Why don't you ask Stacia why she doesn't want me anymore, doc?"

Emily starts singing in my ear so I can't hear what Sam's saying to me or what she says to Stacia. I can see their lips moving, and I think I see Stacia wiping a tear off her cheek. I wonder what Sam said to make her cry, and I get even more pissed off. Who the hell does she think she is? Besides, it's not like Stacia'd care if I really did have a problem. She just doesn't want to get blamed for it when she dumps me. That's what Emily says, and I think she's right.

I'm standing now, tears running down my cheeks, fingers tingling where they touched Emily's smoothly perfect skin. Stacia's got her hands over her face, and I can hear her crying for a minute, until Emily starts singing again. I can see Sam put her hand on Stacia's shoulder. She's looking at me, and her lips are moving, but I can't hear her very well. Emily's pressing herself against me now, grinding her breasts into my back and running her hands over my hips. I can hear Sam using words like *addiction*, but I want Emily too much to really pay attention. I imagine that if I let her do me right here on the table they won't notice a thing, and that makes me laugh. Emily laughs with me.

Stacia takes her hands away from her face and just looks at me. She looks sad and angry, and it pisses me off even more. "I've got a better girlfriend than you now! She wants me all the time!" I scream over the tune that Emily's humming in my ears. Part of me didn't want to say that. That part of me thinks that Emily's bad for me and that there's something wrong with what's going on. I imagine stomping that fear into dust, then sweeping the dust out of my head. Emily loves me. She always tells me so. Her hand slides between my legs, scorching the skin under my jeans. I rock forward against her hand, my eyes closing.

Stacia screams something, then I hear her stomping away. Sam goes with her. Emily's hand stays between my legs while her other hand works its way up my shirt and grabs my tit. I arch my back against her and she sticks her hand down inside my jeans, so loose now they don't have to be unbuttoned. I hear drawers slamming in the other room, Stacia sobbing and cursing, Sam saying something quiet. But Emily's hand is inside me and I don't need anything else. Not Stacia or sleep or food. I can just live on love. I start laughing as the front door slams and Emily rubs my clit just right. My knees are too weak to hold me up, and I fall on the floor, but Emily catches me before I hit the tiles. She unbuttons my pants and drops those red lips to my slit, and I come and I come and I come until I can't move anymore. I ask her to stop and she laughs and she looks for a new way to make my body sing in her hands. I wonder if Stacia could even see me now. Then Emily says she'll stay with me to the end, and I smile at her as I fade away, my hips bucking to the pressure of her tongue.

Neil Kroetsch

Had a Lover

"A few minutes ago Mrs. Fazekas was telling me about her lover," said Arnie as he filled another bucket with clay and handed it to Ralph.

Ralph grunted with the weight. He dragged the bucket to the front of the crawl space, eased his way up and out onto the sidewalk. Then he reached down, pulled up the bucket and emptied it into the big container parked in the street. He nodded to Mrs. Fazekas, the landlady, who sat on the stoop. Then he slipped back underground. He crawled back toward Arnie, who was digging the access tunnel under the house and who had loaded up two more buckets.

"Her lover? She's what, sixty-eight? Sixty-nine? And looks like she's eighty-two. Anyway, even though she calls herself Mrs., she never married. Told me so herself."

"Not a lover now, no. Her lover back in Hungary a long time ago."

"Yeah, like World War I."

"Here." Arnie handed Ralph another bucket, which he dragged out through the tunnel to empty into the container outside. They continued like that for a few more hours before taking a break. Mrs. Fazekas had returned inside her apartment, so they sat on the stoop smoking and resting. Both were in their late twenties and earned their living doing odd jobs.

"I guess I reminded her of her lover back in the day," said Arnie.

"Didn't know you spoke Hungarian."

"Wise guy. She never told you about him?"

"No," said Ralph, "and I've done quite a few jobs for her. Painting, sanding, repointing the bricks. So what'd she say?"

"That he was handsome. Handsome and kind. And passionate."

"Passionate? Guess the old bag's feeling nostalgic and sentimental. Let's finish this gig."

They returned to the basement for a final four-hour sprint, after which Ralph went to the corner store for a six-pack. Muddy and tired, they sat on the stoop sipping a beer.

"Got two jobs for you next week, if you're interested," he said. "Two days loading trucks at a warehouse, and a moving job on Friday."

"Sure," said Arnie. "That's great. Hey, so far 1976 has been a good year."

"Yeah," replied Ralph, "good year for pussy, too."

Arnie adopted a high, breathy voice and said, "Ooo, Ralph-san! Ralph-san!"

They clinked their beer bottles and laughed. The previous week they had gone downtown one night to a bar and met two Japanese women, who invited them to their hotel room. An hour later, after the first go-round, they had switched women. It had been a good night. An insurmountable language barrier—just the way Ralph liked it. No time wasted with conversations or considerations. Or feelings. One day in February he'd met a deaf girl on the subway, and an hour later she was in his bed. Another good night.

"Paid tomorrow, right?" said Arnie. Ralph nodded. "Go out tomorrow night. Get lucky again."

"Hope so." Chances were good, judging by the past three weeks. Tourists were pouring into Montreal for the Olympics, and he and Arnie had enjoyed the charms of a few of them.

Arnie stood, drained his beer and then tossed the bottle to Ralph. "Sayonara, big guy." Ralph picked up the empties and went home.

He returned the next day to get paid. He rang the doorbell, and there she was, slowly making her way down the staircase to the street door, as ancient and dowdy as ever. Frumpy, bland housedress, no makeup, scraggly hair, bit of a limp when she walked.

"Hello, Mr. Ralph." She had never been able to pronounce his surname, so she always called him Mr. Ralph. "Here you go," she said, handing him the cheque, "and thank you."

"You're welcome. Now the plumber and the electrician will have room to work under the house." He turned to go but then Arnie's comments came back to him. *What was it he had said? Passionate, yes.* He turned back to look at her, gazing straight into her eyes. She blushed. He realized that he had never viewed her as anything but elderly, and thus unattractive and uninteresting. She returned his gaze but began blushing again, and lowered her eyes. Ralph felt a stirring, which surprised him.

"Arnie tells me you had a lover."

"Back in Hungary, yes. Long time ago."

"No lover now?"

"No."

"Why not?"

"Oh, Mr. Ralph, at my age..."

"You don't miss it?"

"What?"

"The smell and feel of a man."

"Oh, Mr. Ralph, I..." She caught his gaze but then lowered her eyes. Ralph hesitated, but only for a second. *Why not?*, he thought. He reached out and raised her chin. She gasped, but held his gaze. "Mr. Ralph..." He undid the first two buttons of her dowdy housedress, staring into her eyes all the while. She didn't move, so he undid three more. Still she did not move. He undid the rest and let the dress fall to the floor. She was wearing a full-length slip. He lifted it up and reached inside, stroking her between the legs. She gasped again. Ralph bent down, picked her up in a fireman's carry and climbed up the stairs. He opened the door to the apartment and placed her upright. She was trembling.

"Mr. Ralph, I ... has been so long."

"I'm sure you remember how it's done."

"I ... I must..."

"Visit the bathroom? Sure."

She made her way down the hall to the bathroom and shut the door. Ralph could hear a tap running. He chuckled to himself. *Man, like taking candy from a baby.* He looked around the apartment. The furniture was as drab as her clothing, lightened only by the odd colourful knickknack from Hungary. He tried the first door to his left. It was her bedroom, laid out in a similar flat, listless style—beige coverlet, dark curtains, an armchair most likely purchased at a thrift store. To Ralph, it all conveyed the impression of a life that had stopped upon her arrival in Canada, of someone simply making do, drifting from day to day as though waiting for the inevitable and uneventful end. He stripped, and draped his clothes across the armchair. He lay down on the bed, his penis erect and eager, pleased with himself. No chase involved, an easy lay, tapping straight into an old woman's loneliness.

The bedroom door opened, and she entered. He turned to look. The sagging, liver-spotted skin, the flat, droopy tits sticking to her sternum, the hairy armpits ... *What was I thinking?* His erection rapidly deflated. *Man, I must be out of my mind. I gotta get out of here.* He lifted his torso to rise just as Mrs. Fazekas reached the bedside. Without a word, without sitting on the bed or kneeling down, she bent over. Her mouth engulfed his cock. The pressure, the feel of the saliva and the movement of her tongue had an immediate impact. Hard, Ralph eased back down onto the bed.

She sucked vigorously, hungrily, taking in the entire shaft. Ralph let out a small groan. She then released his cock to swallow his balls. *Man, the old gal's good.* He revelled in the movement of her tongue as she shifted the testicles around in her mouth. She then eased off and raised her head to give him a smile. He smiled back. She placed a hand under his thigh and gently turned him over. Ralph lay spread-eagled on the bed. He could hear her get into position on the bed. *What's she up to now? She ...* "Ahh!" he exclaimed, the sound oozing out of his mouth as he felt her warm, wet tongue penetrate his anus. "Oh, yes."

"You like, Mr. Ralph?"

"I like very much." She probed expertly with her tongue, and Ralph lifted his ass so that only his knees, head, and shoulders were touching the bed. Mrs. Fazekas reached forward with one hand and stroked his cock. Ralph luxuriated in the twin sensations of her tongue in back and her hand in front.

"You think I old, Mr. Ralph? Old and ugly."

"Mrs. Fazekas, I ... Hey, don't stop." She had removed her tongue and her hand.

"Turn over." Ralph obeyed. "I not young, beautiful woman, Mr. Ralph, but am woman. A woman who like men."

"Sure, Mrs. Fazekas. Please, go back to what you were doing."

She slapped him hard across the face, twice.

"Hey, watch it, you old..."

"Yes? Old what? Old witch? Old cow? That what you thinking? Old, dried-up immigrant? Crazy old woman?"

"Man, I don't need this." Ralph rose from the bed and headed toward his clothes on the chair.

Sitting on her knees, Mrs. Fazekas suddenly jumped from the bed, knocking a small picture frame from the bedside table. She fell to her knees in front of Ralph and sucked hard on his cock. Ralph paused. She sucked harder and then pulled away, gazing up at him. "Please, Mr. Ralph,

I sorry. Forgive me. I ... is so long."

Ralph stooped to pick up the object from the floor. It was a frame containing a small photograph, three by four inches, of a couple in their thirties, arm in arm. The woman had her hand draped over the man's wrist and was smiling at the camera. The photo was wrinkled and faded, as though handled many times before being placed in the frame.

"Budapest, 1939."

It took Ralph half a second to grasp the name of the city, for she pronounced the *s* as *sh*. *Budapesht*.

"And that was the last..."

"No," she said, taking the photo and placing it back on the bedside table. "I see him one more time. 1946. Back from Russia. From camp."

"Camp?"

"Prisoner camp."

"Oh, prisoner-of-war camp."

"Yes. But he not the same ... He ... So ... So, I come here. To live."

To live, thought Ralph, gazing at the mottled prewar wallpaper, the window that hadn't been opened in at least a decade, the floor in need of finishing. *No family, no friends. Came here to mark time, to subside, to watch life drift away.*

"Mr. Ralph, I not had a man since..."

"Since when?"

"Since twenty-nine years."

"Twenty-nine ... Since leaving Hungary. Shit. That's a bit too needy for my tastes."

"I angry, because I old and you young. You strong, you good-looking. I hit you, is stupid. Forgive me."

Ralph reached for his clothes. She raised an arm and tossed them to the floor. "Please, I am old, but I ... I want you, Mr. Ralph." Ralph gazed down at her, unsure of how to respond. She took it as a cue and stroked his erection with her hand. "You make an old woman happy, yes? What you like, Mr. Ralph?"

"I like what you were doing."

He made his way back to the bed and resumed the crouched position, ass in the air. She licked his asshole fervently, stroking his dick at the same time.

"You like?"

"Yes, I like."

"What else you like? Please, Mr. Ralph, tell me."

He turned over and looked at her. She was now so eager to please, so nervous. So vulnerable and so desperate, it made him hard.

"You have margarine in your kitchen?"

"Yes."

"Go get it."

She stepped out and returned with a margarine container. He didn't have to say a word. She dutifully buttered his cock and then lay face down on the bed. He took the margarine and placed some on his finger. He shoved it up her ass. She whimpered. He extracted the finger, dipped two fingers into the container and shoved them up her ass. She gasped but remained still. He moved his fingers back and forth and also in a circular pattern, all the while watching her face for her reaction. She said nothing and remained perfectly still. He then removed his fingers and placed generous amounts of margarine on his prick. He eased the tip of it into her asshole carefully, and she caught her breath.

"Yes, Mr. Ralph," she gasped, but he could see tears welling up in the corners of her eyes. He continued nonetheless, slowly forcing his cock all the way up her ass. She gasped repeatedly. He didn't care.

"Oh, Mr. Ralph."

"Shut up. Not another word."

He pushed steadily in and out, changing the rhythm every minute or so to enjoy her whimpering and the changes in her breathing. And her tears, which were now flowing freely. He came in a hard, brutal finish and sighed deeply. He remained seated on her, watching her as she sobbed quietly. Then he rose and dressed. He made his way to the door.

"Mr. Ralph?"

He turned to look at her. *Man, what was I thinking?*

Robin Evans

Priorities

Jack drops by with a bottle of whisky and a couple of flaps of cocaine. He's always doing thoughtful things like that. It's part of our long, drawn-out courtship: coke and booze instead of flowers and candy. I do my little happy dance, shake off my hangover, and feel alive, like I'm ten years old. The powder is crunchy, dirty-looking stuff—definitely not the best money can buy. A few lines and my nose will be raw. Still, we chop it up fine and set up a few rows. Settle into our domestic bliss.

My apartment is stifling. I open all the windows, but there's still no breeze. A shiny layer of sweat settles on our skin. It isn't long before Jack's tugged off his clothes, and, in the spirit of things, I do the same. We lounge around naked on my Oriental carpet, and I wonder aloud why we haven't slept together yet.

"Priorities," Jack says. He stretches his toes to touch mine and then leans back spread-eagled in front of me.

Jack has a beautiful body, caramel skin with just a few blond hairs sparkling down his chest. His tattoos are Japanese-style. One arm is covered with vines and water lilies, while the other has a chubby kid being chased over his tricep by a determined orange carp. His back, though, is what really gives me shivers. From tailbone to shoulder is the shell of a huge snapping turtle, all reds, yellows, and oranges. Its webbed claws embrace his hips and shoulders like it's riding piggyback. The turtle's head twists over Jack's shoulder, and its beak—terrifying in black, green and purple ink—bites into his neck, just missing his Adam's apple.

I saw the turtle in a dream once. Months later it turned up on Jack's back in glowing technicolour. Ever the romantic, Jack had the tattoo artist hide a shadowy "Lorelei" in one of the turtle's eyes.

"I've always wanted to sleep with you, though," I say through grinding teeth. I'm not sure if I mean it or if I just like the way it sounds. I stretch out on my stomach, prop myself up on my elbows, and lick my Oxford dictionary clean of the last remnants of cocaine. "Let's do a coco puff, Jack. Let's get really truly blindly fucked."

Jack's sitting up now, his eyes slightly glazed, the pupils huge. The beginnings of a drug-induced erection blossoms between his crossed legs. He absently tugs at his penis and then pushes it out of sight as he looks me up and down.

"God, you're beautiful, Lorelei." He grabs my ankle and pulls me closer. He runs a finger up my leg until I can't stand it and kick out, shivering with goosebumps despite the heat. "Such a tease, though." He laughs, then releases me as if my flesh burns him.

I watch Jack roll a cigarette back and forth between his fingers, loosening the tobacco. He taps some more coke onto my dictionary, and sucks it up into the smoke. My mind is wandering; my high has settled in, and I begin to feel beautiful again. I admire my body, the curve of my stomach below my bellybutton, the dark triangle of hair between my legs that shines blue-black next to my sun-starved skin. I see turtles and lily pads appear; I feel golden hair brush against my thighs.

"Come here, Jack." I press my thighs together and cross my legs, turning myself into a human corkscrew. Jack straddles my waist and puts the cigarette in my mouth. I draw in my breath, once, twice ... and hold it. I feel Jack's hands on my breasts, softly cupping them and rubbing gently back and forth.

"How's that, baby? Feel good?" He leans over me, and I exhale a stream of grey smoke directly into his face. I pass him the cigarette and let my eyes roll back. My body goes limp.

He probably could make love to me now. It is probably the most perfect moment for it. My body enthralled and stupefied at the same time. The drugs tingling through every inch of me. If he fucked me right now, it would be beautiful. Perfect.

But he doesn't. The moment passes, and instead Jack slips the cigarette out of my hand and inhales as deeply as he can. He lets the drug fill him up, and he rolls off me. Both of us lie there on our backs, sweating and shaking through the drug's twisted, intoxicating version of foreplay.

It's not as if we can't have sex high. We've both got our own stories about the things we've done with other people in various states of drugged stupor. In fact, once the cocaine is flowing, sex is all we talk about. There's just something about us. The drug is a perfect chaperone; it keeps us distracted, envelops us in a strange lustful chastity.

30

It takes us a few minutes to figure out what the buzzing sound is. Jack fumbles through the crumpled pile of clothes sitting next to us and finally finds my cellphone. He checks the call display and places the vibrating phone on my stomach.

"It's Danielle." He licks his lips and wipes the hair out of my eyes. "Tell her to bring some beer."

I sniff; residue burns the back of my throat. "Hey, Danielle. What's up, beautiful?"

"I've been waiting for you forever." Danielle is shouting, obviously drunk. I can hear screams of laughter, and music blaring in the background.

"Jack came over. We're just hanging out. Was I supposed to meet you somewhere?" I roll my eyes at Jack and mime lifting a drink to my lips. Danielle is my little shadow. She showed up at an art opening one night and never went away. I like her, though; she's harmless, dependable, devoted.

Jack shrugs his shoulders and turns his back to me. Crouching down, he starts cutting up some more lines on my coffee table. The tail of his snapping turtle twists slightly as he rocks on his heels.

Danielle's still talking. It takes all my energy to refocus on her voice.

"I'm at the Expo beer garden. It's fucking nuts down here; I've never seen so many rednecks in one place in my life. I just spent a half-hour staring at Albert, the world's largest bull. Oh my god, Lorelei, that animal is obscene. It's huge; its penis hits the fucking floor. I'm not kidding."

"I know what you mean." I giggle, but it sounds like some sort of sadistic cackle. Jack stands over me again, his hands on his hips. His cock is still half hard, and he bounces it up and down for me, laughing. "Listen. I'm not going to make it tonight."

"Aw, shit. Am I interrupting something?" Danielle pouts into the phone. I can tell she wants to come over. She's sweet, and she doesn't do drugs, so I can't see a problem.

"No, baby, you're not interrupting. Why don't you come by ... and bring some beer. We'll get tipsy."

Danielle turns up in no time. I buzz her in, and then Jack and I watch her stumble her way up the back stairs. She's carrying a six of Stella in each hand and bounces back and forth between the railings and the wall.

Jack runs down into the stairwell to steady her. He grabs the beer and pushes Danielle forward, making her trip over her sandals. She looks at us quizzically as I shut and lock the door behind her.

"Don't you guys have any clothes? Sheesh. My virgin eyes, really!" Her words are slurred, and she keeps tottering forward until she finally collapses on my couch.

"Too hot for clothes, Danielle," Jack says. "Clothes are overrated anyway." He plucks at her sticky tank top. "Don't you think?" We sit on either side of her and tug playfully at her clothes. Her body stiffens. "I'm not getting naked."

"No, baby, of course not. That's okay," I say. "Jack and I are only teasing."

She smiles then, happy to be the centre of attention now that she's set up some guidelines. Her red hair is plastered flat and her freckled skin is bright pink. It turns white where my fingers touch, but it's hot, burning flesh.

"Uh, so I'm not interrupting, right?"

Jack and I look through her, and both of us speak at the same time. "No," I say.

He says, "You want to do some coke, Danielle?" Jack's finger is still wrapped up in the strap of her tank top. He whispers something in her ear, and she scowls at him and then smiles her big baby grin.

He pulls back and winks at me, but I'm not sure we have enough left to share. "Danielle doesn't indulge, Jack."

"Oh, I don't know, Lorelei. She might want to give it a try. Why not join the party, hey, Danielle?" Jack grabs the coffee table with the coke already lined up and pulls it toward us until it jams against our knees.

"Well..." Danielle looks to me for approval. "Maybe just one line, right? I'm so pissed right now, it couldn't hurt, right?"

"Right. Do what you want." My heart is palpitating wildly. I can't figure out what I'm supposed to be sharing here. I feel suddenly worn out and washed up. I need another line. "Just let me go first, okay?"

I lean over the table and inhale a line in each nostril. Jack gives me a look like he's all of a sudden calculating how much I owe him. He pushes Danielle back and snorts two lines for himself. He sweeps up what's left into a tiny, half-hearted strip and passes her the straw.

With his hand on her back, he talks her through it. Danielle's good at playing the innocent. She holds the straw and turns it up and down in her hand. She grabs her beer and empties it in one gulp. Jack's voice is low and sweet. He holds Danielle's hair to keep it from falling into the coke, and I find myself frozen, fascinated by the way the light plays against the sweat on the back of her neck.

The drugs kick in right away. Danielle's eyes double in size and she starts talking, talking, hyperventilating. I've got my eyes half closed, and Jack's got his hand on her thigh, rubbing it up and down.

"I got a new tattoo. You want to see?" Danielle bubbles excitedly. I kid myself that she's talking to me. But Jack answers first.

"Where is it?"

"Here. It's here." Danielle jumps up and unzips her shorts. She pulls them down until a hint of her strawberry hair shows. There, right below her hip, nipping at her pubic hair, is a beautiful orange and red snapping turtle.

"Oh fuck," I say before I can stop myself. I lean forward and smell her damp skin. Jack leans in, too, and touches her, tracing the outline of the tiny turtle.

I look for its eyes, but can't see my name there, just two black dots.

"Fuck," I say again and cough up some of my beer. Jack's finger is still tracing back and forth while Danielle wavers on her feet, ready to fall.

"Let me get us some more drinks." I need to get out of this room. I need to hide in the cool air of the refrigerator and stop for a second.

In the kitchen, I keep the lights off, stumble around in the dark, and make as much noise as I can. I open cupboards and slam them closed. I recite the names of the rotting foods in my fridge. Finally, I count to one hundred, grab three beers, and walk back into the living room.

Danielle and Jack are sprawled naked on the floor when I walk in. Fucking. She has her eyes closed, demure as always, and her teeth are clamped around her hand, to keep from calling out his name, I suppose. In between Jack's thrusts, I can just see her tiny turtle, while the one on Jack's back fills the room. It's hard to see anything else.

Jack gets on his knees and grabs Danielle's legs, tilting them up until only her shoulders and head remain on the floor. Her pussy stares up at me from that angle, and I can't help but touch her lightly. I trace her tattoo and slip my finger down until I can feel Jack's penis straining against my hand; I slip my finger inside Danielle's cunt to be next to him the way I want to be. I lean over, and he kisses me hard, biting my lip.

He doesn't make a sound when he comes. He just stops, then lowers Danielle to the floor. He rolls away from her, and finally she opens her eyes. She's embarrassed to see me hovering over her, but I reassure her, shush her, and kiss her flushed cheeks.

Danielle squirms a little, her face the darkest pink I have ever seen. Her eyes are welling up, and they search mine, waiting for me to tell her that we're okay. I stare into her and force myself not to blink. Her face starts to flinch uncomfortably and her mouth teeters on the cusp of a nervous smile. I know it's up to me how this thing goes. Poor Danielle is just waiting for me to make up my mind. I make her wait for it. I drag it out. When I finally give her the tiniest smirk, it's as if she's coming again; the look on her face is pure rapture.

I lean over and grab Jack's pants from our pile of clothes on the floor. Digging through the pockets, it doesn't take long to find what I'm after. I pull out one last sneaky flap.

Jack grabs my ankle as I walk by. "Have I told you lately just how fucking beautiful you are, Lorelei?"

I dangle the flap over his nose and poke him in the ribs with my foot.

"Dirty boy," I tease. "If you and Danielle are done..."

Jack shrugs his shoulders. He sits up and presses his face into my pussy; his hands clawing their way up my legs.

"Danielle who?" He grins at me and tries to grab the coke from my hand. "I've only got eyes for you, Lor, you know that."

I wag my finger at Danielle as she pulls on her tank top. "Good. Because there's definitely not enough here for all three of us. Come on."

He follows me into the bedroom and locks the door behind him.

MARK PATERSON

The IGA Kissing Bandit

They needed to get Luke done up like a girl because they wanted to get the IGA Kissing Bandit, really fuck him up.

They went to Sylvester's. Everybody knew he was converting his parents' basement into his own salon, preparing to go full tilt into the business just as soon as he got his cosmetology diploma from the professional program out of the high school.

Sylvester's mother, green robe and no eyebrows, face pale, half-hiding behind the front door, said Sylvester was still in bed. Larry convinced her they were his friends from school, all four of them, and that he wouldn't mind being woken up.

Sylvester didn't bother to change out of his nightclothes, a baby-blue sleeveless T-shirt and grey sweatpants with the waist cord missing, and sleepily escorted the guys down the creaky stairs to the basement. He pissed in the little bathroom down there, listened to them jumping around in his half-finished salon, guys who were certainly not his friends, guys now imploring him to do the job on Luke. He flushed the toilet and scratched his head, dug a crusty sleep crystal from the corner of his left eye.

Somehow, these guys felt it was okay to ask him to do a job on Luke. Even more distressing was the fact that somehow, someway, Sylvester felt it was okay, too. He could hear them beyond the bathroom door, in *his* salon, laughing and mocking him even now, now when they needed him. He turned on the tap but didn't put his hands under the water, out of spite.

With Sylvester in the bathroom, Luke slid into a salon chair installed in the concrete floor of the basement, rested his hangover on squeaky maroon vinyl, and watched the other guys inspect the place. Mikey jumped up, clumsy in Kodiaks, and took hold of a wooden beam in the unfinished ceiling. He swung his body and hoisted his legs up, dangled upside-down like a kid on the monkey bars. "You're gonna kill yourself," Larry said. But he lost interest and joined Dean in jeering at the posters and pinups covering three of the walls, all images of men with good hair. Rick Springfield in the early 1980s. Keifer Sutherland in the late 1980s. Arsenio Hall in the early 1990s. George Clooney in the late 1990s. John Tesh in an indistinguishable era.

Luke swivelled in the salon chair and faced the fourth wall, a floor-to-ceiling mirror with a white melamine shelf installed horizontally along its length, waist-level. He checked his reflection, thought he looked pretty good in his jeans, even sitting. He was happy with the progress of his hair, blond tresses finally beginning to reach his shoulders, knew it would look fabulous in his hockey helmet, and knew to pretend not to know. His eyes looked tired, a little glazed. They'd all had plenty to drink the night before, Luke especially; liquor had helped conceive the plan to get the IGA Kissing Bandit, and more liquor had helped celebrate its conception. He closed his eyes, headache raging, and hoped Sylvester would throw them out, so they could all just forget about it.

The bathroom door opened with an airy sound like an armpit fart, and Luke turned his head, saw Sylvester coming out. Dean hopped over and crouched beside the salon chair, fooled with the levers. There was a click. The chair reclined sharply and violently, giving a little bounce when it reached its limit, with Luke horizontal, his hair giving a little bounce, too. The other guys laughed. Howled. Mikey dropped from the beam, fell on his ass. More howling. Luke giggled, too. He saw Sylvester march over, disappear behind him, and with a quick jerk Luke was sitting up straight again. He felt like he was in a dentist's chair. Sylvester was reflected in the mirror, professional-looking behind the chair. Stubble dotted his face, heavier in the moustache area; he looked angry, peering over the top of Luke's head. Luke searched for other things for his eyes to look at and found the toes of his running shoes in the mirror beneath the shelf. On the shelf between a hairdryer and a jar full of scissors and combs, a little clock radiated 9:49 AM in red digital characters.

Larry pulled a wad of bills rolled up with a red rubber band from his jeans pocket, waved it at Sylvester. "So how much is this going to cost us?" Ten seconds of silence. "We're going to *pay* you," he said defensively.

***

They pulled into the IGA parking lot a little before noon, all of them bouncing around in Dean's mom's forest-green Windstar, Luke amazed they'd come this far. The plan was a good joke, a scenario to laugh about. Even while he was in Sylvester's chair, looking up at pink skin tags scattered among the future beautician's brown armpit hairs, he kept waiting for somebody to call it off. And even after the makeover was complete, he didn't think they'd actually go to the grocery store. But here they were, backing the minivan into a parking spot near the back of the lot, with an unobstructed view of the store's entrance and exit doors.

The cackling was wild, fever-pitched, when the IGA Kissing Bandit finally emerged with a customer, a pudgy woman wearing a purple sweatsuit; she was in her early fifties, with black curly hair and huge sunglasses. The Kissing Bandit had his green IGA windbreaker on, unzipped, grocery apron showing under it. He was probably twenty-five years old, dark stubble high on his cheeks. Short black hair standing up straight in the front, gelled like a pro. A light brown birthmark on his left temple. He followed the woman to a section of the parking lot off to the right of the minivan, one brown paper grocery bag and a jumbo box of laundry detergent nestled in his cart.

"What a skank," Larry scoffed from the passenger seat in the front. Luke laughed. He was pressed up against the side window in the back, Mikey behind him trying to get a good look outside. The tissues and cotton balls that stuffed Luke's bra mingled with the hairs on his chest, tickled him.

"Doesn't matter," Mikey said, straining to look over Larry's shoulder, practically humping him in the excitement. "He'll do it. Skank or no skank. He'll do it no matter what."

The purple-sweatsuit lady pointed to her car, and her purse strap slid off her shoulder, down her arm. She opened the purse with her other hand—maybe the whole motion had been on purpose, Luke speculated. Or maybe the strap had simply slipped. Luke wondered which it was, felt he should know the answer for sure before heading out himself. It might be important.

The woman opened the back of a light-blue Chevette. The Kissing Bandit put the detergent in first, then the paper grocery bag. He raised one arm in the air, clasped the hatch with his fingers. The lady reached out with a closed fist toward the Bandit, in offering—obviously money, but it was impossible to see how much. The Bandit's other arm went straight out, palm up and outstretched, a gentle snatch. A quick deposit into his apron pocket and he looked to one side, the other, the first side once more, and then his head bobbed forward like it was popping out of the water doing the breaststroke, and his lips were on purple-sweatsuit lady's lips. The Windstar exploded with a cheer, the boys jumping up and down, whacking each other like caged monkeys. After a few high-fives, a couple of hoots, and some considerable pounding on the back of the front seat's headrest, Luke glanced toward the Chevette again. The hatchback was closed, the Bandit was pushing his cart back to the IGA entrance, and the lady was fumbling with her car keys without actually looking at them. Her head was motionless, fixed in a straight-ahead stare, dazed.

The guys started chanting his name. "Luke! Luke! Luke! Luke!" It was actually going to happen. Larry turned around and handed him the remainder of the cash, the red rubber band a little slack now. When they had put the funds together at Dean's the night before, all the guys throwing money into an old Blackhawks hat while the spliff made the rounds of the room, Luke didn't think it was really going to happen. Even when he agreed to be the mark, his long blond hair making him a natural for the role, Luke had no doubt the plan would fall apart. It was ambitious, too ambitious, yet typical of their sauced imaginations, and he put his twenty bucks in the cap confident they would wind up spending the money on more beer and more grass the next night.

Larry pushed the cash into his hand. "There's still enough for a two-four, but get other stuff, too—broccoli, meat—make it look good. Make it look real."

To Luke there was little more real than the erection that he'd had almost constantly under his skirt since his first glance at himself all done up in Sylvester's mirror.

He stepped out the minivan's sliding side door, feeling his friends' encouraging slaps on his shoulders and back. He strategically placed Dean's mother's old purse before his crotch and turned to face the guys one last time before going in. Larry lit a cigarette and tossed the burnt match out the front passenger window. "Remember," he said, a little cloud of smoke with each syllable, "we're right here. Right behind you. Make it look good. Do your part and leave the rest to us." Luke nodded and turned, made for the IGA entrance. He stumbled a bit in his heels.

It was a cool day, mid-October, grey sky. Orange and yellow leaves whipped by his feet, carried by a crisp wind. Many long and boring school weeks still lay ahead, but Christmas vacation was kind of coming up. Luke held the image of his own snow-swept street, his house and his neighbours' lit up for the holidays, until his hard-on began to deflate.

Sylvester sat in the back of the Windstar, behind the driver's seat, his legs and arms crossed. He concentrated on staying quiet, making himself small, invisible. He didn't want to be there. But when they asked him to come along he'd said yes automatically. He was ashamed now for the gratitude he'd felt at the invitation. He didn't want to be there but somehow couldn't get himself to leave. Couldn't move.

Larry turned around and leaned into the backseat area. "Y'wanna a smoke, girly man?" he asked, extending his pack. Sylvester reached for a cigarette impulsively, feeling that gratitude he hated again, said thank you as sarcastically as he could muster, and accepted Larry's match. He blew smoke out his nostrils and looked at the road beside the IGA parking lot. Cars passed, the trees were bare, grey swirls of smoke escaped chimneys of houses. He tried to follow the road with his eyes as far away as he could.

Luke spied his own reflection in the big window next to the automatic doors and slowed for a closer look. He got excited fast; a quick intake of breath, a shiver all over. It was maddening, confusing, but he couldn't look away. He was so convincing. Black low heels (still feeling quite high to him) that his feet had slipped into with surprising ease. Black skirt, the hem well above the knees, a good portion of thigh showing. White blouse, long-sleeved because he had been willing to shave his legs but not his arms—with small, gold-coloured buttons outlined in black, done up to the top to play it safe. The Kleenex and cotton balls, however, gave him a beautiful pair of breasts with, thanks to Sylvester's diligence, a slight upward curve, not too small and not too big. "Just perfect for kneadin' and rollin'," Dean had joked, almost too lavishly, as the guys looked Luke over in Sylvester's basement. And Luke felt bad for all the times he'd called Sylvester names, to his face and behind his back, because faggot or not he had done an amazing job.

His blond hair was pinned flat in the front with pink and purple barrettes; in back it curled out slightly on both sides. His makeup was subtle, realistic—just a dash of lipstick, a dusting of mascara, nothing overdone. He twisted slightly and nonchalantly inspected his ass in the black skirt. He felt sexy. His erection pressed his underwear taut. Along with arousal, however, came an eerie sense of grief, a deep burn in the base of his throat. Somehow, as he stood there staring at the girl in the reflection, admiring her, he was also mourning her. Mourning a girl who had not died but who would never live. A girl he would never meet and who would never meet him, not without the barrier of reflective glass between them, never to touch, to connect. Shielded behind the purse, Luke passed through the automatic doors and into the IGA.

He caught his first stare early in the vegetable aisle. It was an ugly guy dressed all in blue denim, red baseball cap and bristly stubble dotting flabby cheeks and a double chin, loading up on the complimentary coffee. Swizzle stick stuffed in the corner of his mouth like an old cigar, white crud on his bottom lip, his face lit up as Luke pushed his empty shopping cart past him. Without even looking back, Luke could feel the twin laser beams of the guy's stare trained on his hips and ass, hated and loved it at the same time.

Sylvester asked Mikey to slide the side door open and he tossed his smoked cigarette outside. "Actually," he announced, "you know what, guys? I gotta go. Thanks for everything, but I gotta get home."

"Whoa!" Dean said, turning around in the driver's seat. He motioned to Mikey with his chin and the sliding door was quickly shut. "Don't you wanna see if it works? This is, like, your work on the line, man. Don't you wanna see what happens?"

I'm afraid of what's going to happen, Sylvester thought. He crossed his legs and made himself small in the back seat again.

In the cereal aisle, Luke took to swaying his hips slightly with each step. The skirt slid gently up and down his thighs, barely an inch each way, seemingly designed for this kind of motion. Not only men but women were checking him out now. Mere glances from the front, fleeting and subtle, but from behind the stares were searing. Luke glanced back once in a while to watch the ladies look down or away quickly, embarrassed.

He reached for a box of Cheerios and tossed it in his cart. It looked lonely in there with the broccoli. He reminded himself to make it all look real. He added a box of Frosted Mini Wheats. At the end of the cereal aisle he caught a man his father's age ogling his legs. Impulsively, Luke raised his skirt a little, pretended to scratch an itch on his left thigh. His admirer whistled exaggerated appreciation. Luke blushed.

He turned his cart right, right again, up the pasta and cake mix aisle. He increased the sway in his hips just a bit. Leaning his arms on the shopping cart handle and pushing it forward at the same time, he turned to see the man following, smiling with his eyes half closed, conspiratorially, unafraid to look right at him. Then a "Look out!" from in front, and there he was, the IGA Kissing Bandit.

He cradled a stack of dented tomato sauce cans with his arms and chest, steadied it with his chin. "Almost had a collision there," the Bandit said with a smile. Then a wink. "I'll see you later?" Another wink and a sideways nod of the head at Luke's shopping cart. Luke silent. Heart in his throat. Dampness in his armpits. Heat on the back of his neck. Couldn't stop staring at the Bandit's lips. Dry-looking, not much darker than the skin on his face. A cramp low down in Luke's stomach. He pushed his cart forward, felt the IGA Kissing Bandit's stare, but he didn't dare look back.

"What's taking him so long?" Larry asked nobody in particular, frustrated, feet up on the dashboard. He lit another cigarette. "It's not that complicated, groceries. Let's get this show on the road for fuck's sake."

Sylvester took a deep breath. "What exactly is going to happen? You guys have some kind of plan?"

Larry turned his head, smoke escaping his mouth like a fog. "Oh, yeah. We got a plan." He high-fived Dean. Mikey chortled. Sylvester looked at the road again.

Luke was fourth in line at one of the cash registers, and he saw the IGA Kissing Bandit leave the store with a tall woman's groceries in his cart. "Bitch," he couldn't help but think. He was happy, though, felt the timing was just right for him to wind up with the Bandit.

But it wasn't, not exactly. The lady in front of him, perhaps sixty years old, with an order consisting mainly of tuna fish cans and frozen vegetables, was ready to leave when the Bandit returned to the store. The Bandit automatically began walking toward her. He even started to smile at her. Luke stared at him while loading his groceries on the rubber conveyer belt. The Bandit's eyes met his. Luke shivered at what seemed unsaid. The Bandit squeezed by the old lady and helped Luke lift a case of Molson Dry from the shopping cart to the conveyer belt. "See you in a minute," the Bandit whispered, then disappeared up the bread aisle.

Luke dug into the bottom of Dean's mom's old purse. It was empty save for the roll of bills with the red rubber band. He was short two dollars. He asked the cashier to remove the Frosted Mini Wheats from his order. He was owed change. A nervous-looking teenager with a single shiny red zit on his chin bagged Luke's groceries, paid Luke little heed. The stares of others, however, customers and employees, were undeniable. His order all set to go, and the Kissing Bandit appeared, seemingly out of nowhere. A wink. Luke fell in beside him like it was something he did every day, matched his steps and listened to his small talk. Smiled. Shrugged. Glanced.

"Okay! Here they come, Jesus fuck! Hide!" Dean shrieked. Mikey jumped up on the back seat, crouched and held his knees, bayed like a dog. Larry told them both to shut up.

Sylvester craned his neck to see out the front windshield. He felt proud and sick. Luke was stunning. The IGA Kissing Bandit couldn't keep his eyes off him. Sylvester was more confident in his abilities in that moment than ever before. This was better than a diploma in cosmetology. This was real life. And that's what made him sick. The *real life* part.

Luke pointed to the Windstar. He tried to make his voice soft. "Over there." He looked down, smiled, stole a glance at the Kissing Bandit. The Kissing Bandit winked again. Luke stared at his lips. He had to avoid them. The guys had to act before it happened. They'd promised.

The Kissing Bandit asked Luke his name. "Lucy," he replied.

"You live around here, Lucy?"

"In the new development behind the mall," Luke invented. The Bandit asked Lucy if she was new to town, then. Luke cleared his throat and answered yes, she was. The Bandit told Lucy about the great new inline skating rink and adjoining movie theatre down on Lobo Road. Luke said, "Wow," half-expecting to be asked to the entertainment complex on a date, half-disappointed when he wasn't.

Luke directed the Kissing Bandit to the back of the Windstar. He opened the hatch. "You really should keep that locked, you know," the Bandit said, mock scolding, a wink and a smile. Luke smiled back. The Bandit placed the groceries in the van, one bag at a time, buffering them finally with the case of beer. They closed the hatch together.

"Okay, it's closed," Larry whispered from the floor of the front seat. "What're they doing?"

Mikey peered over the back seat, not raising more than his eyes above the vinyl. "They're just standing there. Looking at each other."

"Well," Luke said, pausing. "Thank you very much."

"You're welcome," the Bandit said, magnanimously. He clasped his hands together and rested them at the centre of his waist, looked down and to the side.

"Well. Thanks again." Luke took a step forward. He dropped his eyes, shyly. He looked up, utterly uncertain of what to do. He had to get the Bandit to try and kiss him. That was the plan. The Bandit goes for it, and the boys jump him. He had to get him to make a move. "Well," Luke said again. He looked shyly at the ground. "Um," he laughed nervously. "Um, aren't you going to—?"

The Bandit cleared his throat. Luke looked up. The Bandit bobbed his chin, pointed with it at the purse. He raised one eyebrow, waiting. Luke's erection rested against the side of the purse, out of sight. He reached into it carefully, never moving it from its place. He extracted the change. Two dollars and six cents. He handed it to the Bandit.

"Thank you very much. It was nice meeting you, Lucy." The Bandit walked backwards against his cart, pushing it along, waving bye-bye.

"But—"

"Just so you know," the Bandit said, hushed, checking around, "you're about eight bucks short of, um, the VIP treatment." He puckered his lips and kissed the air, winked. "See you next time." He turned around and, placing his left foot on the lower bar of his cart, pushed off repeatedly with his right foot, rolling back to the IGA as if on a scooter. As he neared the entrance he stepped up with his right foot, rode his momentum, then leaned his body a little to the right, and the cart turned accordingly. The IGA Kissing Bandit disappeared back into his store. A grey-haired lady with a single plastic grocery bag dangling from her hand paused in the doorway to watch him go by.

The guys poured out of the Windstar. Larry kicked the parking lot pavement. Dean said, "Fuck." Mikey burped and said, "Fuck," too. Sylvester poked his head out the open side door. Luke felt his erection fade.

"What the hell happened? What did you do?" Dean asked him.

"It costs like ten fucking bucks to get him to kiss. I didn't know!"

"Then why didn't you give it to him for Christ's sake?"

"I didn't have enough!"

"Aw, shit. This fucking sucks." Dean dug into his pocket. Came away with lint and a dime. "This really sucks. You guys got any money?"

"Forget it, Dean," Luke said. "Let's get out of here." He put the purse on the ground—it was safe to let go of it now—and started undoing his blouse buttons, anxious to get to his real clothes in the car.

"Don't do that out here," Sylvester advised from the van.

"Who asked you to talk, you stupid fuck?" Dean barked, approaching the van with a sidestep, his chest out, as if he'd been challenged to a fight. "Fucking faggot. Nobody told you to talk, nobody cares what you have to say."

"Leave him alone, Dean," Luke said, tired. Tired of it all.

"You gonna let that faggot tell you what to do?" Dean shot back, seemingly ready to fight Luke now. He grabbed his crotch and his voice came out overdone falsetto: "*Don't do that out here.*" He skipped closer to Sylvester, started sparring. Punches whistled past Sylvester's ears, each one closer than the last. He cowered deeper into the van. The other guys laughed. Luke's hangover returned with renewed and stifling vigour.

"I'm telling you, Dean, just leave him the fuck alone."

"*Somebody's* ass is gonna get whupped today," Dean sang, his tone somewhere between gangster movie and professional wrestling interview. He started cuffing the sides of Sylvester's head, softly at first but with growing intensity. "Supposed to be the IGA Kissing fuckin' Bandit, but I'll beat on this candy ass if I have to."

Luke stopped working at getting his blouse off. He walked over to the scuffle and got behind Dean. He inserted both forearms under Dean's armpits, linked his fingers behind Dean's neck—full nelson applied—and lurched his buddy up and away from the van. "I said leave him alone," Luke grumbled, releasing the hold.

"You looking to get your ass kicked now?" Dean challenged. "Eh, fuckup?"

Luke turned and walked away from Dean, toward the minivan. Mikey and Larry were already climbing in, climbing past Sylvester. Luke stretched out his hand. "Somebody wanna give me my clothes?"

Dean blindsided him waist-high with a hip check, and he was down on all fours on the parking lot pavement, right knee and elbow stinging. He looked up and saw Sylvester being pulled from the back seat of the minivan, a look of utter shock on his face. Dean deposited him unflatteringly on the ground.

"The two of you can have a good old time and fuck each other up the ass," Dean spat, dismissing them as he hopped into the driver's seat. He started up the engine and called out the open window: "Get the fucking Bandit to join in—make it a three-way, you fucking faggots." He peeled out, tires shrieking.

Luke got himself to his feet, watched Dean's mom's minivan lurch out of the parking lot, wheel up the street. "My clothes?" he yelled, in vain. "Assholes."

He offered Sylvester a hand to get up off the ground. They said little to each other as they walked back to their part of the neighbourhood. Along the way the blisters started, so Luke took the low heels off and continued barefoot. The forest-green minivan returned, slowing abreast of them, horn bleating, the cackling resonating, Mikey hanging out the front passenger window with a camcorder, Larry in the back window with a moon.

"Nice ass," Sylvester offered, deadpan, only loud enough for Luke to hear.

Luke chuckled. He adjusted his skirt, pulled it taut. Checked himself out and smiled. "Not as nice as mine, I'll tell you that much. Not as nice as mine."

Ashok Banker

Serpent's Tale

Anish heard the cobra before he saw it. For a brief beery moment, he thought the hissing was just the sound of his urine falling into the shrubbery. But then he opened one scrunched-up eye, squinting against the gaudy afternoon sunshine, and saw movement. He opened the other eye as well and peered into the leafy dimness of the thicket into which he was relieving himself.

That was when he saw it. The flat, shiny head swaying gently like a banana leaf in the breeze. The beady dark eyes. The tapering stalk of its body. And slowly, drunkenly, he recognized the unmistakable shape of a king cobra.

He stood mesmerized for several seconds, his urine flow hesitating once, twice, then cutting off abruptly. His bladder was by no means empty—there was still at least half of the six-pack left to go. But the thought of standing with his penis exposed to the swaying head and flickering forked tongue of one of the world's most poisonous snakes was not an appealing one.

A memory flashed through his alcohol-addled brain—the time he had been caught urinating against the wall of a pub in Crouch End, London. He had been fined £200 for that offense. But back here in India where even policemen often relieved themselves at strategic spots on public streets, it was impossible to prevent public urination completely. So Anish was struck with the idea of planting snakes at tempting public spots. Yes, snakes! The prospect of being nipped in the privates would certainly dissuade even the most prolific public urinators. Especially since Indian men usually crouched to relieve themselves, which would put the shameless bastards at eye level with the police serpents!

The image of a dhoti-clad bhaiya squatting on a sidewalk, removing his member, and starting to relieve himself blissfully before looking up, just in time to spy the cobra lunging at his face, was so vivid that it sent a shiver of laughter through Anish.

The cobra rose higher, swaying vigorously now, and slowly began to spread its hood. The hissing grew louder, now sounding like rain in a palm grove.

Anish choked on his laughter. Suddenly, the joke was on him: he was the dumbass caught with his dick in his hand and a cobra preparing to give him the worst blowjob imaginable. The cobra had risen to about six feet, a couple of inches higher than Anish himself. The spread hood was a deep jade-green, almost jewel-perfect in its colouring and sheen. Two symmetrical eye-like markings to the left and right created the eerie impression of a face staring back at him.

As Anish watched, frozen, it began flashing its fangs at him, its tongue flickering sibilantly. Its swaying slowed until the snake was almost motionless. Dappled shadows of overhead leaves made it almost invisible now. *Protective colouring*, it was called. Only its eyes, glinting in the tiny arrows of sunlight that pierced the thicket, revealed where it was.

Suddenly, he had no more memories. No smart ideas. No funny incidents.

Just a dry mouth. Swirling nausea. And in his hand a shrivelled member that he didn't have the courage to replace and zip up.

The cobra lunged.

He opened his mouth to scream.

The cobra fell directly at his face, mouth open wide, fangs glistening with venom, jaws spread so wide he could see into the pink-black hole of its throat. Into the belly of his death.

He shut his eyes, feeling the world reel in a final vertiginous roll that was as much the result of too much beer and exhaustion as sheer terror.

A searing heat struck his face. His cheeks, mouth, neck, and upper arms and chest—almost bare in the slender cotton vest—were splattered with a surprising wetness. He felt the burning of the fangs as they sank deep into his cheek, one penetrating the edge of his lower lip with the smooth sharpness of a needle passing through wool.

And then he heard the echoes of the gunshot fading away.

He opened his eyes. And saw the ichor on himself, on his arms. His left eye was blurred by something gooey and icky. His lip was heavy with more of the stuff. The burning on his cheek and lip weren't caused by puncture wounds but by hot viscous fluid. An acrid, ammoniac stench filled his nostrils.

He felt movement to his left, and then Irfan passed him, thrashing through the shrubbery to the spot where the cobra had stood. He examined the ground carefully, the revolver held loosely in his hand.

"There," Irfan said, pointing to Anish's feet.

Anish looked down, still too stunned to speak or react.

He saw the remains of several eggs. Oddly shaped eggs, longish rather than oval, almost angular at the ends. He had seen them before in documentaries on *National Geographic* and the Discovery Channel: snake eggs.

"You fucked up its nest," Irfan said.

Then he looked up at Anish's face. And grinned.

"Better not lick your lips, man. That isn't pussy juice on your ugly mug!"

The other guys roared when they heard the whole story. When Irfan described how he'd approached Anish from behind and seen him standing and staring into the shrubbery, they lost it totally.

"You should have seen him, man. The behenchodh was standing there with his dick in his hand, winking at the fucking cobra! I think he was trying to make a pass at it! Right, Anish?"

Sanjay slapped Anish on the back, hard enough to make him spill the water he was using to wash himself. "Kya yaar, Anish? I thought you only tried goats and sheep when you were desperate. I didn't know you had a thing for snakes too!"

Anish shoved him away angrily. "Fuck off."

Michael winked at Sanjay. "Come on, man. Have a heart. He just saw his girlfriend being shot dead!"

That broke them up. Sanjay slapped the side of the Mitsubishi van several times, unable to stop laughing. Michael held his head and laughed till tears ran down his cheeks. Irfan grinned as he loaded a new bullet into his revolver to replace the one he had used.

Jaspal's voice cut through their laughter. "Okay, okay, guys, enough is enough."

He caught Sanjay's hand as he was about to slap the van again. "Relax, bhai. Maybe the next time you're pissing and a ten foot cobra jumps at you, we'll see how big your balls are, okay? But right now, give Anish a break. The fact that he's not collapsed shows that he's tougher than he looks. Give him some credit."

Anish looked at him gratefully. Jaspal winked at him reassuringly. The Sikh was as big-hearted as he was big.

A truck rattled past them, heading slowly up the ghats. Anish squinted at the hills ahead. The countryside was dry brush as far as the eye could see. But at the top of those hills, he could glimpse green. The green of the Khandala plateau where they had been heading before they pulled over for this pit stop.

The guys were grumbling about Jaspal not having a sense of humour. Jaspal opened up the ice box and cracked open some more beers. He tossed frost-encrusted cans to waiting hands. The grumbling stopped instantly. The popping and fizzing sounds of cans being opened were followed by the tangy rusty-iron odour of chilled beer.

Jaspal offered one to Anish, but he shook his head. His lip still felt a little numb where that snake goo had splattered. Although of course, he could use a little forgetful-medicine to take his mind off the incident. He was having a hard time shaking off the memory of the cobra lunging at his face.

Jaspal yanked open the driver's side door. "Hey, guys, if we've all finished our little encounter here, let's proceed to our destination. We've still got a weekend to spend celebrating!"

Sanjay and Michael whooped in unison and high-fived one another. Irfan grinned at Anish as he got into the back seat of the van.

Anish was the last to get in. As he bent his head to get into the van, he glimpsed something out of the corner of his eye. He paused and glanced toward the spot where he'd encountered the serpent.

Jaspal honked, revving the van's engine. "All aboard, guys!"

Anish got in and tried to shut the door. He didn't pull it hard enough for it to catch. His limbs felt weak, watery.

Irfan leaned over him to pull the door firmly into place. He spilled a little beer on Anish's lap. It felt hot rather than chilled, although Anish knew it was ice cold.

"You okay?" Irfan asked.

"Just a bit spooked, that's all."

Irfan nodded. "Don't blame you, man. That must have been one heck of a moment. As I came up behind you and saw it about to spring, I wished I had my camera. It would have made one hell of a wide-angle shot."

Anish grinned weakly. Irfan was a cameraman. They worked

together a lot.

"Glad you had that instead of the camera," he said, pointing at the revolver lying on the seat between them.

Irfan patted it affectionately. "You bet, man."

Jaspal had waited a few moments to let a caravan of freight trucks pass, heading downhill. The Western Express Highway was the major conduit for goods coming into Bombay from various other states, and the heavy vehicle traffic was relentless. When the last of the convoy had passed, Jaspal pulled away from the dirt shoulder and, taking them onto the blacktop, picked up speed as the van carried them effortlessly up the steep gradient.

Anish glanced out one last time and blinked, startled.

For a moment, just a fleeting instant, he thought he spied something long, greenish-black, and serpentine emerging from the grass behind them, at the dirt shoulder they had just vacated.

He turned to Irfan to ask if he had seen it, too. And found the cameraman offering him a fresh can of beer.

"Take a brewski, chill," Irfan said.

Anish hesitated, unsure whether to tell Irfan what he had just seen. *If* he had seen it. His nerves were jittery as a schoolgirl's on a first date.

Then: "What the hell," he said. And took the can.

The queen cobra watched the human vehicle disappear up the hillside, spewing its toxins into the air. She had seen the one she sought, staring out of the moving box at her. Her sharp eyes had recognized him. He was the one whose image had been imprinted on her mate's mind at the moment of his death. The one responsible for his brutal murder, and the destruction of her unhatched progeny. If she had been in the nest at the time of the attack, she had no doubt that the human would have attempted to kill her, too.

But he would have failed.

Because she was a queen cobra. Mistress of the forest floor. Sanctified ruler of all that crept and crawled. Anointed by Lord Shiva himself.

And even the most powerful species in creation crossed her path at his own peril.

She hissed and raised herself, turning this way and that to decide how to proceed next. Her hood flared, partially opening to reveal a breathtaking corona of colours. She was the finest of her breed. Just as her mate had been the greatest of his lineage. His loss would be unbearable. It would take her seven hundred rebirths to find a mate as perfect, as well-suited. Seven hundred lives of sadness and longing and loneliness. Seven hundred lifetimes alone.

The human would pay for his murderous act.

Raising herself to her full height—a formidable seven feet—she sent up the mantra of invocation. Calling on the Lord and Master of the Snake Tribes. Shiva himself. Asking him to grant her the power to fulfill her only desire.

Revenge.

She examined herself in the full-length mirror and was pleased with what she saw. She was beautiful. In the human sense of the word. By cobra standards, she was an ugly biped. But to sexually active human males she was irresistible. That had already been proven by the way that trucker had repeatedly glanced sideways at her on the ride here, by the heads that had turned—female as well as male—when she had walked into the resort hotel, and by the effortlessness with which she had talked the pair of humans into letting her into their nesting place. They were mates, a male and a female. It had been easy to tempt them with her irresistible sexual allure.

But it was only now, seeing her reflection in the mirror, that she was able to fully appreciate the perfection of her transformation. Truly, Shiva was a great Lord. He hadn't just created the Cobra, most lethally beauteous of all species on Earth, he had also invested a chosen few with the magical power to transform their shape in times of need or danger. She had been born with this power in her blood, she knew, yet it was one thing to be aware of it, and another thing altogether to see its magic at work.

The naked body reflected in the mirror was a model of human perfection. From the way the two humans had stared at her as she disrobed, she knew that she was irresistible now. She had the ability to get close to the human male she sought, to gain his trust completely. Killing him would be child's play now. She smiled at the tiny gnats buzzing ecstatically around her breasts. "Go," she whispered to them in their insectile language. They went to do their work, finding the remaining humans, biting them, softening them for her.

She glanced at the two bodies lying sprawled across the double bed.

Their skins had already turned bluish-white from her venom. It reminded her of the human artistic depiction of Lord Krishna she had seen in temples in the forest. The Blue God, he was called. He had turned that colour after being bitten by the Snake Goddess he had fought as a child—or so said the legends of her kind. The mortals, of course, had their own theories; but to the serpent folk he was the beautiful venom-blue Krishna.

She cupped her breasts, marvelling at their weight and shape. Perhaps this form wasn't as ugly as it had seemed at first. She ran her palms down her flat, undulating abdomen, down to the triangular darkness between her thighs. Her fingers felt the wetness and heat there and came away dripping milky moistness. She tasted it and shut her eyes, relishing the pungent flavour and odour of her own venomous secretions. Yes, not so bad at all.

Perhaps she would dally with a few more males—maybe even a few more females—before she completed her mission of vengeance. After all, it was the cobra custom to mark the passing of a mate with an orgy of ritualistic copulation. The primordial, frenetic urge to ensure procreation when faced with death and singularity.

Tonight, before she accomplished her revenge, she would leave many more humans gasping with pleasure—and pain. Then she would turn them all into blueskins. Unlike the young, divinely blessed Krishna, none of them would survive.

They drank themselves into a stupor in the bar with the glorious view of the valley. The monsoons had left the entire plateau lush and rich with greenery. Waterfalls plunged from the tops of cliffs, carving their way down the sheer rocky slopes to shatter hundreds of feet below in a fine mist of spray. Enormous flocks of birds darkened the purple-streaked skies as the sun set, looping around the valley as if searching for something. Monkeys leaped from tree to tree on the hills below, chattering excitedly. Anish assumed that the general disturbance was due to sunset. Still, it was one hell of a hullabaloo, even seen from the soundproofed vantage of the resort hotel.

Something prickled the hairs on the back of his hand. He looked down and saw a tiny insect scampering away. He would have slapped it instinctively, but his reflexes were sluggish, unresponsive.

"Wow, man," Irfan said about a million times. "Great location, man.

Really great."

Jaspal smiled indulgently, exchanging a glance with Anish as they noted Irfan's five-hundredth repetition of the litany. Sanjay and Michael had vanished to eff-knew-where.

Anish could see that Jaspal was pleased at the compliments. His firm had designed the hotel. Not Jaspal personally, but his brother and father. "Best resort in Khandala," he had said proudly. And from what Anish had seen so far, it was.

Irfan put his hand on Anish's shoulder, squeezing gratuitously. "We should shoot here, man. Got to shoot this place. What say?"

Anish nodded. "Yeah, it's terrific. But what do we shoot here?"

He was wondering if maybe Irfan was gay. He had never known him to touch so much. Then again, he had never seen him this smashed before either.

"Anything, man! There must be some sucker of a producer we can talk into letting us shoot a couple of episodes up here. Just look at the view. And the light is maha-perfect. Magic light. Oh, man, look at that shot right there."

He got up and went closer to the semi-circular picture window, banging his head against the glass as he leaned forward to catch the "shot."

"Wow, man," Anish heard him say again, and he and Jaspal grinned lazily at one another. If Irfan were a camera, he would have been totally out of focus right now.

Sanjay returned from wherever it was he'd disappeared to. Michael wasn't with him. Sanjay looked like he'd been up for three nights drinking. He was excited about something. "You guys want to sit here drinking all night, or you want to really party?"

Jaspal looked at him. "You're the one who wanted to just stick to this air-conditioned box. I told all you guys: let's go for a swim and cool off."

"I'm not talking about swimming, bro. I'm talking about some real fun. Are you in or out?"

He emphasized the last three words with a suitably illustrative gesture: making a circle with his forefinger and thumb and then poking his other forefinger through the circle. *In. Out.*

Irfan looked intrigued. "Dude," he slurred drunkenly. "Are you, like, talking about what I think you're talking about?"

"Oh, shit," Jaspal said. "Don't tell me."

"Pussy, bhai! Pussy time! Who wants to party—and I mean, *partay*! All those interested please raise your dicks!"

"Chill, guys," Jaspal warned, glancing around. "The whole staff knows me. I told you: no hanky-panky here."

"So who's doing anything here?" Sanjay said. "Let's shift this unit into my room. That's where the main feature presentation's waiting for us, bro!"

"In your room?" Irfan asked suspiciously.

"Yeah, man," Sanjay said. "Michael's already getting his whistle wet while we're standing around here jacking off dry-handed. Wait till you see her, guys." He again made an *O* with his thumb and forefinger and repeated the in-out gesture. "Class act."

Anish frowned as they navigated their way out of the bar and through the foyer of the hotel. "You've got a whore in your room?"

Jaspal groaned and slowed down. "Guys, guys! I told you back in Bombay: no whores!"

Sanjay clapped his hand on Jaspal's shoulder, trying to give him a shove. Their size difference was so immense, it came off like an infant patting his father's arm. Jaspal's burly Sikh frame didn't budge a millimetre. "Who said anything about whores, bro? This is a real live nymphomaniac we've got here."

Jaspal cocked an eyebrow at him doubtfully. "Pukka? Sure, na? Because I don't do whores, man."

"You better believe it, yaar," Sanjay said, and they resumed their way shakily down endless carpeted corridors.

A trio of cherubic little girls in swim trunks, all carrying identical purple rubber floats, ran by squealing, chased by a single harried, overweight mother with a towel wrapped demurely around her torso. "Ashita, Rashita, Nashita, you stop right now or I'm going to slap all three of you!" A burly, hairy, pot-bellied father waddled slowly after her, sucking on a Bacardi Breezer. He burped as Anish passed him. Anish distinctly heard him say, "Squeeze me."

Sanjay was hyping the nymphomaniac. "Yeah, bro. You should have seen the way she came on to us, she was ready to do it right there and then on the spot. But we said we've got to give our buddies a share of the pie, too."

They reached the Suite Royale. Jaspal's family contacts had gotten them the suite for the weekend virtually for free. That was why they were here. That, and to celebrate Anish's serial getting a thirteen-episode extension.

"Now listen, bro," Sanjay said in a stage whisper. "This dame is hot enough to burn your skin off, okay? So we'll all get our shot at her, okay? But since Mike and I found her first, we're getting first crack. He's doing her already, and I'm next. Clear?"

Jaspal and Anish exchanged glances, eyebrows raised. Then Anish nodded, Jaspal shrugged. What the hell.

Irfan called out from up the corridor. "Hey, man. Wait up. I'm part of the scene, too, remember?"

He caught up with them and put a hand around Anish's neck, caressing him with a little more affection than Anish needed to feel. "What's happening, man? Is this a gangbang or what? Fuck, I wish I had my camera."

Sanjay shushed them as he started to turn the doorknob. "Get ready to meet the Queen of All Pussy."

He opened the door to the suite, and they all trooped in.

Anish retched dryly, heaving until his abdomen muscles ached. If Jaspal hadn't been holding him up, he would have collapsed on the floor. As it was, he was shivering with exhaustion after the violent vomiting.

He raised his head, leaning against the cold tiled wall of the toilet stall. He tried to tell Jaspal it was alright, he was done, but couldn't get the words out of his bile-seared throat. He stared through tear-distorted vision at the Sikh.

Jaspal smiled down at him. "It's okay, bhai. I've seen puke in my time, too, you know. Nothing to be embarrassed about. You're just having a very bad day, that's all."

Anish cleared his throat, spat into the bowl, flushing for the nth time. "I'm making you miss the party."

Jaspal grinned. "What party? A gangbang with some desperately lonely housewife? Once those guys have drunk enough, they'll fuck a hole in the wall, yaar. I bet you a thousand bucks she looks worse than the whores who stand on the street in downtown Bombay."

Helped by Jaspal, Anish made his way shakily to the washbasin. "Nobody can look worse than those whores, man. I can't even believe they have the guts to stand out there and solicit customers." He ran water and began washing his face and hands, using his finger to clean his gums, which felt scuzzy.

Jaspal laughed and leaned against the wall. "They're just earning a living. But can you believe the desperate idiots who actually have sex with them? And pay for the filthy privilege? It's unbelievable, I tell you. I'd rather die than even touch one of those dirty bitches."

Anish caught something in his voice, a bitter intensity that was stronger than the comment warranted, and glanced up briefly from his washing. He saw Jaspal staring at something. It took him a moment to realize it was his own ass.

He put both hands on the washbasin, supporting himself, and stared at the Sikh. The tap, still running at full force, splashed a steady stream into the porcelain basin. The front of Anish's shirt was soaking wet.

After a second or two, Jaspal looked at Anish. Their eyes met in the mirror.

The brief but unmistakable flash of hungry longing on Jaspal's face was a revelation to Anish. "Jesus, Jassie," Anish said, turning to his friend. "I never knew you were queer."

An instant before he embraced Jaspal, he noticed the tiny insect bite on Jaspal's neck. It was identical to the tiny bite he'd got in the bar and, like his own, had turned faintly bluish.

Irfan came out and joined Michael and Sanjay on the balcony. They had dragged two single couches out and were sitting with their feet up on the balustrades, smoking and drinking. Irfan looked for a place to sit, but there wasn't any.

"Fuck, man," he said, and slumped to the ground in a cross-legged heap. "Fucking sucked me dry, the bitch."

He nudged Michael. "Give me a fag, bastard."

"Ask nicely, maderchodh."

"Fuck you, behenchodh."

Sanjay murmured: "When you two cocksuckers have finished insulting each other's mothers and sisters, maybe someone can help me figure out where our great director-saab and the great Serd have vanished?"

Mike chucked a crumpled pack of Marlboros at Irfan. Irfan took the last one and chucked the box over the railing. It hit Michael's foot and fell back in Sanjay's lap.

"I saw Anish looking like he was about to puke his guts," Mike said. "Jaspal must have taken him to the loo."

"There's a loo in here," Sanjay said. "Why go to the hotel toilet?"

"Would you want to puke when your friends are banging a bitch in the next room, man?" Irfan asked, his customary drawl stretching like a waistband that had lost its elasticity. "I told him to fuck off. It's a real downer to smell puke when you're trying to get a hard-on."

"What do you mean *trying*, man? With that cunt in there, you don't have to try. She sucks it so well, it stays hard even after you've come. If you guys weren't waiting in line, I'd still be in there, doing the rumba-sumba with her."

Irfan plucked the Marlboro pack from Sanjay's lap and threw it at Michael. It hit his head and went over the railing, disappearing into the darkness of the valley.

"Why don't you go then, go back to her. She's still hungry for more."

As if on cue, the woman appeared at the door of the balcony. She was naked, but the billowing curtains concealed her lower half. Irfan squinted in the darkness, trying to see her more clearly. Now that he had fucked her, she didn't look half as shapely as before. But she wasn't half bad either: no Mallika Sherawat, maybe; then again, which other Indian woman could measure up to that high standard? Actually, come to think of it, she did have something of the Mallika glamour; there was that very nicely toned body, the broad hips with the flat abs, and those breasts, oh God, those breasts were to die for. The whole package was pretty damn good after all, good enough to make his cock twitch once, then stir sluggishly like a sleepy snake warming itself in morning sunlight.

"Andar aajao na," she said in Hindi in a whinging, mock-shy voice. "I thought you were going to bring all your friends to have fun with me."

"Yeah, sure, cunt," Mike said. "We've put a notice up in the lobby. Party in Royale Suite, all are invited. Stag only!"

They cracked up over that one.

The woman waited another moment, then, when none of them moved to get up, she came out onto the balcony and sat on the arm of Michael's couch. Her very nicely shaped hip jostled his arm.

"Fuck, bitch! You made me spill my beer!"

But she had her hand down his boxer shorts and was massaging him to an erection. After a moment, his groaning turned to moaning.

Sanjay and Irfan watched and smoked. Sanjay licked his lips and nudged Irfan. "Ever tried a three-way, yaar?"

"No, man. And I'm not going to try it tonight either. You go ahead. I don't need to fuck her again—or watch you guys fucking her."

Irfan rose to his feet, staggering with exhaustion and alcoholic stupor. "I'm going to figure out where our other two buddies disappeared to." He heard the valley below explode in a flurry of animal, bird, and insect cacophony. It sounded like a predator had found its prey.

Anish and Jaspal stumbled into the room in the darkness, pulling one another's clothes off with feverish hunger. The Sikh's hands were all over Anish, and Anish groaned as the big man's powerful arms held him.

"Whose room is this, Jas?" he managed to ask through his passion.

"Hotel staffers use it to change, shower and all," Jaspal breathed into his ear. "That's why I know the door's kept unlocked."

Anish was about to ask him whether he had remembered to lock it after they came in. But then he saw the bed and froze.

"Jas," he said, grabbing his friend by the shoulders. "Look!"

Jaspal turned and saw the two naked bodies, a man and a woman, on the bed. Their blue-tinged skin and wide-open staring eyes left no doubt about their condition.

"Shit, they're dead, yaar!"

"What happened to them?" Anish asked, backing away toward the door.

"God knows, yaar," Jaspal said, going over to the bed but not touching the bodies. "Hey, I know these people. She's the assistant hospitality manager, and he's the F&B steward. They must be—"

The room door slammed shut with a deafening impact.

Anish swung around. And saw a woman standing before the closed door. A naked woman. With beady black eyes and a bindi on her forehead that looked like a third eye staring at him.

She smiled, and her tongue appeared briefly, flickering in and out, forked and hissing.

Anish felt the same bone-freezing chill that had paralyzed his body at the moment the king cobra had struck.

Suddenly he had a feeling that his very bad day was just about to come to an even worse end.

***

By the time Irfan found them, she was done with Anish and was humping Jaspal. The Sikh was already turning blue from the venom in her vaginal juices. He turned his head, gasping, and stared at Irfan with blurry eyes. But Irfan's eyes were fixed on the woman squatting above Jaspal.

As her sexual ecstasy grew, she shivered between human and reptile form, unable to maintain the integrity of either body. At the instant that Irfan stumbled into the room, she was neither wholly human nor cobra. The smooth, dusky skin had turned scaly and shiny; the black hair had turned into something that was almost a hood.

"Come on in," she sussurated. "Join your friends."

She shot out a leg that was almost a tail, catching him behind the knee and knocking him to the ground, flicking away the revolver that he clumsily tried to remove from his waistband. He tried to scramble away but felt the leg change shape, turning into an appendage that writhed and tightened around his leg, dragging him in.

Despite himself, Irfan had an erection. The creature impaled herself on him, and her venomous juices seared his cock.

Irfan saw her maw open, revealing those two terrible, impossibly large, gleaming white fangs, dripping white, pungent, semen-like venom, and he understood it all in a flash: the cobra they had killed, the ancient Hindu legend of the nagin that assumed human form and wreaked revenge on the humans who had killed her mate.

The last thing he saw before the world turned white was a reflection of himself, terrified, in the iridescent opals of her serpentine eyes. In the reflection he was turning blue, blue, so blue...

DAN RAFTER

The Adventures of Ultima

When Celia received the powers of Ultima she expected to make headlines for saving the world, for tossing supervillains into prison, for rescuing innocents from blazing buildings.

Instead, here she was, captured in her first encounter with a real supervillain, tied in chains and helpless. Father Simmons, the priest she was supposed to rescue, was lying bruised and bloody on the floor, surrounded by the Eel's henchmen.

The Eel, dressed in her skintight green-and-purple costume, brushed aside a strand of Celia's long brown hair and blew into her ear. The Eel's tongue lightly licked that same ear, making Celia jump as a spark of electricity gave her a small shock.

"Why don't you break free?" the Eel asked, stepping away from her captive. "Surely the chains I've wrapped you in aren't strong enough to hold the mighty Ultima?"

Celia struggled, flexing her muscles. But the chains wouldn't budge. It was hopeless. Her battle with the Eel had drained too much of Ultima's power.

The villain grinned as she stared at Ultima's bound body. Celia saw the villain's eyes linger over her chest, especially. And why not? Her tits were magnificent—firm, round, and straining to pop out of the spandex that barely held them in place. They were still a shock to Celia, who had grown up flat-chested.

The Eel ran her whip up the front of Celia's costume, stopping to run tiny circles around the nipples poking the fabric. "So delectable, really. It's a shame you're on the wrong side."

Celia felt the heat rising in her body, her nipples hardening, the power of Ultima starting to surge. But not enough to both free herself and fight the villains.

Celia had first become Ultima just three weeks earlier. She'd returned home from the sex shop with a bagful of new toys; she was especially excited about one of them in particular. Buried underneath a pile of extra-large rubber dildos, she'd stumbled on a blue and white vibrator with a weird design. She was immediately drawn to it, like it was calling to her, somehow. The clerk didn't know how to price it—it had no tag—so he'd offered it to Celia at a bargain.

When Celia got home she had to get at that new vibrator, and quickly. She held the blue and white toy in her hand. She licked her lips and felt the heat spreading from between her legs. With her arm she pressed her small breasts against her chest. She twisted the vibrator's bottom, and it started to buzz.

Before she could use it, though, a genie—big and blue, with white shorts—popped out of the vibrator in a puff of smoke. Celia tried to scream, but her voice wouldn't work. She wanted to run, but her legs had turned to stone. The genie didn't have much to say: "You are the chosen one: Ultima! Say the magic word, 'Amitlu.'" Then the genie disappeared. So did the vibrator.

Celia thought she had lost her mind. But she gave the genie's magic word a try. "Amitlu!" she yelled. Sure enough, in her own puff of blue and white smoke, Celia changed. Her body was now encased in a shiny spandex suit, a suit so tight it wrapped around her body like masking tape, highlighting each and every curve. And what curves! Suddenly Celia had breasts—giant pornstar breasts. But these weren't plastic. They were 100 percent real.

She had to touch them, had to run her fingers over their magnificent roundness. She couldn't resist. As she did, her nipples poked through her spandex, and they, too, were incredible, so large and inviting. She was a superhero now: wasn't she supposed to be virtuous and pure? But she tugged at her top until the spandex slid down. Once she'd freed her tits, Celia couldn't stop herself from pulling at their erect nipples, sliding her hands into her cleavage, and squeezing her breasts until she gasped.

Celia was no virgin, but never had she felt such pleasure. The sensations that ran through her body nearly knocked her to the ground. She leaned against the mirror, her hot breath misting its glassy surface.

She needed to get at her pussy. Still leaning against the mirror, Celia hurriedly peeled herself free from her blue-and-white spandex. She took a step backwards and stared at the reflection of her new body, naked.

Incredible.

Her hair was long now, not short like she usually wore it, and it shone. Her eyes had turned a deeper green, and they, too, had their own unnatural glow. Muscles rippled beneath the skin of her shoulders and her arms. She turned and gazed backwards at her reflection. Her calves were so strong now, so firm. Her ass was perfect. She ran her hands across it, immediately sending more heat through her body. She groaned, pulled her ass cheeks apart ever so slightly, and slipped a finger between them. As her fingertip brushed against her anus Celia cried out and grabbed the wall to keep, once again, from falling. Her body shook, and she felt the wave of an oncoming orgasm.

Somehow Celia fought it off. She didn't want to cum, not yet.

She felt something amazing, though, as those waves of pleasure buckled her body. She felt stronger, even more powerful than she had just a few seconds earlier.

She spun back around and stared again at her magnificent breasts: they pointed straight at the mirror; they didn't droop, not a bit. Their brown nipples formed nearly perfect circles. When Celia again put her hands on them, her body shuddered, the hairs on her arms standing up.

"Jesus," she said. "This feels so good."

Again she steadied herself against the wall before taking a long look at her pussy, covered with wavy brown hairs and sopping wet. She imagined what it would be like to slip her fingers in there.

The sensations were incredible, as Celia discovered when she slid that first finger between her lips. "Oooh," she groaned. She pushed in another, and the sensations grew only stronger. She let herself sink slowly to the ground.

Before she even hit it, the orgasm came. She screamed and threw her head back, as her whole body shivered and buckled.

When it was over she felt as powerful as a tank. She pulled her fingers out of her pussy, stood up, faced the wall and took one swing. Her fist pushed through the plaster as if it were paper. Then she floated, first just a few inches from the ground, then all the way to the ceiling.

"I can fly! I can fucking fly!"

Water started to fill the locked room. "Shit!" Celia said. "She's gonna drown us!"

Celia strained at the chains that still held her tight. Her muscles ached. This should have been easy—would have been easy if the Eel hadn't drained so much of her power. Celia almost felt like a normal human being.

While she struggled, the priest, who was lying on a metal cot, an arm thrown over his face, groaned in despair.

Heroically, Celia shattered her chains.

"Thank God," she gasped.

She was even weaker now. She took a swing at the steel walls. Nothing happened. She punched harder, still nothing. She, and Father Simmons, were trapped.

She turned to the priest. "Father?"

He raised his head. "Look at what I've done."

"Yes, Father. But I have to ask you something. I can get us out of here. But it's going to take something..." How to say it? "Something ... Well, you may find it a little strange."

"This is all my fault," Father Simmons said.

Celia snapped her fingers in front of the priest's face. "Father! I'm talking to you."

The priest shut his mouth and looked up at Celia.

"That's better," Celia said. "Now, as I was saying, I'm a superhero, and I can get us out of here, but it's not going to be easy. It may make you feel a bit ... uncomfortable. Perhaps you should turn around."

And with that, Celia leaned against one of the steel walls, pulled the top of her spandex suit down, and let her breasts spill out.

Father Simmons gasped. Before he shifted his legs, Celia thought she noticed his bulge getting just a bit bigger.

Ultima could smash through walls, fly through the air, run fast as lightning. The whole bit.

She had only one weakness: Celia quickly ran out of energy, and, as she discovered, the only way she could recover it was to get hot—sexually speaking. She gained strength by rubbing her cunt, by massaging her tits. But she gained the most whenever she reached orgasm—then her power rushed back like a hurricane.

Fortunately, her first few adventures were simple jobs, robberies by petty crooks. She concluded each of these cases before entirely losing her powers.

Word spread of the new superhero in town. She even made the lead story on the evening news more than once.

Ultima was a superstar. No-one had the chance to get a photo, though, and the artist's rendering they used wasn't up to par. They got Celia's new breasts right, drawing them like watermelons stretching against her uniform. But her hair wasn't the right shade of brown, and they made her eyes blue.

The next time Ultima took to the skies Celia made sure to hang around long enough for the cameras. As the flashbulbs popped and the cameras rolled Celia stuck out her chest and batted her eyes. For extra effect, she shook her hair and smiled.

"Tell the bad guys that there's a new hero in town. Her name is Ultima!" she announced before flying into the clouds.

Two days later, the news announcer broke into the middle of Oprah with a breathless report: "Ten minutes ago, the notorious Eel blasted a hole through a historic landmark: the oldest church in the city, St. Sebastian the Healer. She is believed to be holding captive a priest, one Father Simmons."

The camera zoomed in on a gaping hole in the side of the church's wall. Celia dropped her soup on the floor and yelled "Amitlu!" In a flash—well, after sneaking out the back door of her apartment, running quickly down the hall, and rushing down the stairs before any of her neighbours could see her—Ultima took to the skies to battle her first supervillain.

The water was moving fast now, nipping at her ankles. Celia knew their time was growing shorter. Celia resisted the urge to play with her breasts and went right to her pussy. As usual, the first finger sent waves of pleasure rocketing through her body. But, and this was disturbing, not much happened. She felt a bit of energy seeping into her muscles, but it was more a trickle than a flow, and it wasn't nearly enough to bring her back to full power. It was far less than she'd need to get out of the Eel's trap.

Celia dug deeper and inserted another finger, then a third and a fourth. "Yes. Yes," she sighed.

Out of the corner of her eye she noticed Father Simmons shifting his legs again.

Celia leaned against the wall and grabbed her tits with her free hand, squeezing and pinching at her nipples. But she needed more than just a quick masturbation session to power up sufficiently. Celia turned her green eyes toward Father Simmons.

***

Celia had flown into St. Sebastian's ready for another easy victory.

"Look at you," the Eel said when Celia entered the church. "You're a lot better-looking than those other superfreaks I have to fuck around with."

Celia couldn't help but appreciate the compliment. Her new-and-improved chest swelled.

The Eel stepped close. Never taking her eyes off Ultima's breasts, the villain ran her long fingers down Celia's sides. Celia felt the villain's breasts—smaller than her own, but still firm—press against her. Eel bent her head toward Celia's ear. "I can feel your nipples getting hard, sweetie," she said.

"No!" Celia shouted. She delivered a two-fisted blow to the Eel's face, sending the supervillain tumbling to the ground.

"What have you done with Father Simmons?"

"My henchmen are ... interrogating him," said the Eel, getting back up on her feet.

"What do you want from him?" Celia asked.

"The Golden Host. He won't tell me where it is, but I'll find it. And with it, I'll rule the world!"

"Not likely!" Celia yelled, slamming another fist into the Eel's face. This blow sent the villain flying through the air and into the opposite wall of the church.

The Eel shook her head, wiped a trickle of blood from her chin, and stood up. "You are a feisty one, aren't you?"

Then the villain pulled down her uniform top, letting her breasts poke out.

"Like these?" she asked.

Celia, to her shock, did. As she stared at the Eel's nipples the villain pointed her fingers at Celia.

"I'm an electric Eel," the villain explained to Celia.

The air sizzled.

Any good Catholic knows what the host is. Even bad Catholics like Celia knew: it was a piece of bread—or, these days, a flat, tasteless circle—that's supposed to represent the body of Jesus. It's a very holy thing, and good Catholics line up for it every Sunday.

The Golden Host? That's entirely different.

When Celia woke up bound in chains, the Eel gloated, in that way supervillains love to do. Whoever possessed the Golden Host would be able to control nature—to summon thunderstorms, earthquakes, and tornadoes at whim. The Eel wanted it.

And, according to the Eel, Father Simmons had it. The priest was an amateur archeologist. He'd discovered the Golden Host during a digging trip to Jerusalem. He smuggled it back home to St. Sebastian's. No-one knew where he'd hidden it. It was only a matter of time, though, before the Eel found it, with or without the priest's help.

Now, Celia had to save the world.

"Father," she said, "would you mind taking out your penis?"

Father Simmons opened his mouth, but only a strangled gasp escaped.

The water was coming in faster now, tickling the backs of Celia's calves. "I don't have time to explain, but this masturbating isn't working fast enough. By the time I build up enough energy we're gonna need scuba gear. I need some visual stimulation." Celia looked at the bulge already pressing at Father Simmons's pants. "And it looks like you've got the goods, if you don't mind my saying so. We can't let that villain get the Golden Host."

Father Simmons stood up, opened his fly, reached inside his pants, and drew out a thick cock, its head a glistening purple ball.

Celia couldn't help herself. "Shit, Father, that's a nice one."

Father Simmons blushed and cleared his throat. "Thank you, child."

"Um, can you take it all the way out? I'd like to see the whole shaft."

Father Simmons let his cock slide all the way out through his fly. Celia licked her lips and fingered her pussy. The priest's cock was at least nine inches long, she thought. Celia stared at the blue veins running down its shaft. She pulled at her nipples as her eyes travelled down to the dense clump of black hair at the priest's crotch.

What a pity, she thought. All that amazing cock wasted on a vow of celibacy.

"Is it working?" Father Simmons asked.

Celia dug her fingers deep inside her pussy. She was soaked, and she managed to fit four of her digits inside. By now, the spasms of pleasure were buckling her knees. "God, Father," she moaned, "you have a great cock."

"Yes. You've said that already."

Celia grabbed at her pussy with her other hand. Somehow she found space to shove two of its fingers inside her cunt, too. "Touch it, Father. Touch your dick for me."

"What? I ... I can't."

"Do it, Father! For ... for the good of the world."

Tentatively the priest moved his right hand across his dick. He made a fist around its shaft and slowly rubbed it up and down. Celia moaned as she watched the head of Father Simmons's dick shrink and expand in rhythm with the priest's rubbing.

"Tell me how that feels," Celia said.

"It feels nice, Miss Ultima." He began rubbing faster. "Nice."

Celia watched the priest's hand speed up. To her horror, she noticed that the water now nipped at her knees. "Father," she said, "don't go too fast. I might need that."

This brought the priest's hand to a stop. "What?"

Celia stepped in front of the priest and knelt in the water. "I have to do this, Father," she said. "Forgive me."

Celia wrapped her lips around the priest's erect cock. "Shit!" Father Simmons shouted.

The cock grew even larger as Celia's tongue moved along its shaft, as her lips sucked at its tip.

"Miss Ultima, this is so ... wrong," the priest said. Celia ignored him and let his cock slip deep inside her throat. She nearly gagged at its length.

"We can't do this," Father Simmons gasped. He grabbed the back of her head, wrapped his fingers in her hair and pulled her mouth harder onto his board-stiff cock.

Celia couldn't answer; the priest's dick filled her entire mouth.

Eventually, Father Simmons pushed Celia's head away. "Is it enough?" he asked, gasping for breath.

Celia shook her head. "Not yet, Father, I'm sorry to say. I need ... more." She lunged for his dick, but Father Simmons again pushed her away.

"No, child."

"But father, we don't have much time for arguing. I need more."

The priest shook his head. "No, Miss Ultima, I don't mean that. I think maybe we need to go even further. I think you might need me to be inside you."

"Yes, Father, yes! Definitely!" The priest stumbled backwards, to the cot in the corner of the room. Celia jumped atop him, spread her legs, and slowly lowered herself onto the priest's fabulous cock. Just as its tip brushed against the lips of her pussy, Celia stopped.

"What are you waiting for?" Father Simmons asked, shouting.

"I want to make sure that you're ready for this. This could be a major sin, right?"

The priest's cock pushed against Celia's pussy. Her legs shuddered at its touch.

"We have to do it, for the sake of the world," Father Simmons said.

"That sounds good," Celia said.

The cock, despite its girth, slid easily into Celia's pussy, the pleasure it sent through her body so intense she nearly passed out. She no longer saw anything: not the steel room, not the rising water, not even the face of the groaning priest.

In her mind's eye, all Celia could see was that giant cock.

Father Simmons, it turns out, fucked like a pro. The pair were in synch immediately, Celia raising her ass in perfect time with the thrusting of Father Simmons's member. With each push, the head of his cock forged deeper inside Celia. She lurched forward, placing her palms on Father Simmons's chest, to avoid falling. This position allowed her to lift her ass higher in the air, and then to slam it down harder on the priest's cock.

"Father ... are you ... alright?"

"I'm great, fine," the priest answered.

Celia pumped even harder. Father Simmons responded for a few thrusts before abruptly grabbing Celia's sides and stopping her.

"Father?"

Father Simmons struggled with his breathing. "I need to ... be careful. I don't want it to happen too soon." Celia smiled, and Father Simmons quickly added, "We need you to be at full power."

"Yes," Celia agreed. "That is true."

Carefully, Celia slid off the priest's cock. It aroused her even more to look at his member soaked wet with the juices of her pussy. She dipped a finger in her cunt, raised it to her lips, and tasted the juices. "Oh, that's so good," she moaned, shoving her fingers back inside of her. With her other hand she reached behind her and rubbed at her anus.

Celia moved to the wall and braced herself, her ass in the air, pointing toward the priest.

The priest lay still.

"Do it, Father!"

The priest stood, gripped Celia's shoulders, then slowly pushed his cock against her ass. At first it wouldn't budge, and the priest was too gentle to force his way inside. But Celia encouraged him: "Get it in there, Father. Hurry." And Father Simmons found his strength. With one massive push, the thick head of his cock forced its way into Celia's ass.

Celia couldn't believe the pleasure. She squeezed her eyes shut and leaned her forehead on the wall. Her arms trembled against the cold steel. Behind her she felt the force of Father Simmons's cock as it thrust ever deeper into her ass. Each push made her scream, and the priest soon was thrusting so hard he was smashing Celia's tits into the wall.

"Father, it's working," Celia gasped, feeling new power surging through her. "I'm getting ... strong."

The priest reared back and gave another thrust, this one the hardest yet. Celia yelled and felt her legs tense, her stomach tighten, and her breasts quiver. An orgasm! she thought. Yes! At last!

Celia whipped her head back and screamed. Her body rippled from her feet clear to the top of her head. And when the last throes of the orgasm finished washing over her, Celia punched the wall with all her might. Following the wave of water, Celia, with Father Simmons still attached to her ass, fell through the demolished wall and into a corridor.

"We did it," Celia gasped, shaking water from her hair. "We're saved."

Father Simmons didn't answer. He kept pounding at Celia's ass.

"Father? Father? You can stop now," Celia said. "I'm back at full power."

Father Simmons grunted and continued his thrusting.

"Father?"

"Hush, child," the priest said. "I'm ... I'm ... making sure you have ... enough."

The priest pushed again, sending Celia flopping onto the ground, her tits sliding on the wet floor. "Almost, my child," Father Simmons groaned.

"Father? I still have to stop the Eel," Celia said. "She might even know we're out."

"Please ... child." Father Simmons pulled Celia closer to him and buried his shaft deeper into Celia's ass. Celia let out a yelp as the priest's balls slapped against her cheeks.

"Christ, Father," Celia gasped.

Celia heard the sound of voices coming down the hall. They were shouting at each other. Fuck, Celia thought, they know we're out.

Three of the Eel's henchmen—also dressed in purple uniforms—turned the corner. When they saw Father Simmons attached to Celia's ass, the three goons skidded to a stop.

"Father?" Celia asked. "We got problems here."

The priest slid his cock halfway out of Celia's ass, stopped, then slammed it back inside. Celia grunted at the force. Shit, she thought, if he goes any deeper, he's gonna shove that cock outta my mouth.

The henchmen hadn't yet recovered from the sight. Celia decided to take advantage of that and slowly lifted her front off the ground. She shook her tits back and forth. "C'mon, boys," Celia purred. "There's plenty for everyone."

The henchmen first dropped their guns, then their pants. Three erect dicks marched toward her.

So predictable, Celia thought, stifling another yelp as Father Simmons slammed back into her ass. There was only one problem: what was she going to do with three?

Two of the henchmen stopped in front of Celia, waving their cocks (which, Celia had to admit, were pretty big and not bad-looking for henchmen's) in front of her face. The tip of one of them already glistened, and Celia could smell its salty odour. "Guys," she said, "how about letting me give you two the most amazing blowjobs you've ever had?"

She reached her head forward and gave each of the cocks a quick flick of her tongue. She noticed the men's legs shudder.

The two thugs looked more than eager for a blowjob—their dicks were pointing to the ceiling, after all—but they also seemed nervous, so Celia eased their fears. "Don't worry, boys," she said. "Your boss won't ever have to find out. It'll be our little secret. If you've never had a superhero give you a blowjob, you've never had a blowjob." She batted her green eyes. "And you don't have to worry about who goes first. I can fit you both in at once. No waiting."

That sold them. But as the cocks came closer to her lips Celia wondered if she could really make good on her boast.

Meanwhile, the third goon hurried behind Celia. "Out of the way, holy man," he said, giving the still-thrusting Father Simmons a shove. "I want in."

Celia glanced behind her to see the priest give another thrust. Without taking his eyes off her perfectly sculpted ass, he swung his right fist into the goon's chin. The henchman crumpled to the floor.

Turning her attention back to the others, Celia discovered that she could, indeed, fit two dicks in her mouth, even those of the extra-large variety.

"Shit!" the goons shouted simultaneously as Celia slurped at their members. "I'm coming!" yelled the first. "Me, too!" shouted the second.

Celia gulped down the streams of sperm. Even though the thugs worked for the Eel and were, therefore, reprehensible pieces of crap, their cum tasted awfully good.

As Celia spit the two dicks out of her mouth and wiped her lips with the back of her hand, Father Simmons's cock pushed deeper still, pressing against the walls of her ass. Then it jerked three times before the priest let out a massive groan, sending a hot shower into Celia's anus.

"That should do, my child," Father Simmons said drowsily. "That should be enough power."

"I'll say," Celia said. But Father Simmons didn't answer. When Celia turned she saw that he was sprawled on the floor, snoring, his amazing cock already shrinking. All the henchmen were out cold, too.

As Celia stood, small rivers of semen dripped down the insides of her thighs. Celia wiped her hand in one of the streams and popped her fingers into her mouth. She ran her tongue along her index finger, swirling it around the tip.

Celia's pleasure was short-lived. She heard the clapping sound of high-heeled boots coming from down the hall. This was quickly followed by the Eel running around the corner, blue crackles of electricity popping from her purple boots as they clanked against the wet ground. "No-one gets out of my trap!" she shouted.

She slammed to a stop when she saw Celia's naked body. "Holy shit," she said.

Celia quickly bent down to pull up her costume. The Eel gasped. "Wait!" she shouted. "Don't do that."

Celia stopped. She noticed that the Eel was staring at her huge tits and their rock-hard nipples. She followed the villain's eyes as they travelled down, stopping for a just a few seconds at her perfectly flat stomach before coming to rest at her cum-drenched cunt.

"Oh, my," the Eel said.

Celia smiled at her enemy. She slowly ran her hands up her body, stopping to cup her breasts, moving on to pull at her nipples. The Eel dropped her whip and slipped her hand between her own legs. Blue sparks of electricity popped from the villain's fingertips, and Celia sniffed a burning smell in the air.

Well, Celia thought, this might be easier than I expected. "Come here, Miss Eel," Celia said, spreading her legs wide.

As the Eel began pulling herself out of her purple costume, Celia grinned. This super-charged villain, she figured, would be on the floor in a matter of minutes.

Then the Eel's tits popped free. Celia felt a familiar heat between her legs.

Well, she thought, putting her own hand between her legs, maybe it'll take just a bit longer than a couple of minutes.

Soon Celia and the Eel were embracing, Celia's tongue forcing its way inside the villain's mouth for a long, deep kiss. Sliding a finger into the Eel's pussy, Celia whispered into her foe's ear, "What about the Golden Host?"

"Fuck it," the Eel said.

Celia grinned. Case closed.

Sucksluts Anonymous

"Hi. My name is Michael. I'm a suckslut."

"Hi, Michael!" booms a chorus of male voices.

Michael is standing at a lectern positioned at twelve o'clock in a circle of folding chairs in the yellowed basement of a UCC Church. On the wall hang children's drawings of the Hindu gods and goddesses. On the folding table, there are Styrofoam cups in towers and burnt coffee. A dense pall of smoke lingers near the ceiling lamps. The other men look back impassively.

Michael is handsome, with a round head, early salt-and-pepper hair, and maybe too much chin. It makes him look cartoonish, like a super-hero. It's his first time at the lectern after listening to others' tales of cock-induced misery—the heartache, the chapped lips, the beloved pet Pekineses ruthlessly used to attract *what's your doggie's name*-type men in the park.

"Here's how bad I am. On my way over here, there was this hot doorman at The Plaza. Tall, dark-skinned—Hispanic maybe. He was wearing one of those frock coats, an old-fashioned bandleader sort of uniform with the epaulettes and the gold braid. Standing, legs apart. A fucking colossus. Thighs like a speed skater. The two sides of his long coat were spread wide. His pants were tight as a bullfighter's. He jerked his head toward the little valet booth, where they keep all the guests' car keys."

One of the men calls out, "Admit you're powerless against your addiction!"

"Submit to a higher power," says Gerry, Michael's sponsor. He's a stern, grey eminence with an oversized mouth.

"I explained to the doorman that I don't suck cock anymore, that I'm going to meetings and moving along on the road to recovery. He hauled out this slender rock-hard member. Eleven inches long. No shit! I've seen a lot of cock in my day. I've sucked off the so-called 'baby's

73

forearms' and the 'donkey dicks.' Trust me. I don't exaggerate. It had a dark, almost purple tip. On the underside was a thick blue vein that had its own pulse. I flicked it with my tongue until the shaft was slicked and shiny. His crotch had a stale, mossy smell from the heat and sweat."

One of the men in the circle of folding chairs interrupts. "That's it," he says. "Bare your..." he takes a long drag on his cigarette before he adds weakly "...soul."

Michael picks up where he was interrupted. "'Stop fucking around,' the doorman growled, 'And suck it.' So I did. I put my mouth over the tip and got down. It touched the back of my throat before I was halfway down the shaft. His cock throbbed and jumped. His thrust cracked my head back against the underside of the counter. 'Touch my balls,' he said. I cupped his sack, lifted his balls, rolled and kneaded. With my other hand, I grabbed the shaft. I did it as much for my balance as for his pleasure. He was pressing against my head, threatening to knock me over."

A few brothers slink in late, wiping the jizz from the corners of their mouths. Someone eases over and welcomes them to the meeting. Not a single one of them catches anyone's eye. Not even the one Michael had just exchanged blowjobs with in the utility closet braves a second glance.

"I dug fingers into his ass crack. He had a real Stairmaster ass. I pulled it apart, slid my fingers into the heat and moisture. My ring finger touched his anus. He moaned and arched back. I pulled him into me, forcing his cock deep into my throat." Michael's hands perform a pantomime above the lectern that every eye in the room follows as closely as a child watching shadow puppets.

"Then he pulled away. He slid the engorged mushroom cap across my glistening lips as he jerked himself off. He was not looking at me so much as at his own member. Then suddenly he spasmed and thrusted. Wet spunk coated my lips and nose and cheekbones. Another spurt reached my forehead, stuck in my hair. Wet, sloppy chunks exploded all over the place; I caught them in my mouth like they were a first snowfall. At that moment, we both heard the voice that might have been speaking for some time already: 'May I have my Mercedes, please?'"

Michael glances at the circle of men. His face is full of rueful shame. "That's how bad I am. I truly am a suckslut. I admit it: I've lost control."

Faces in the front row nod in recognition. Sympathy. Someone walks over to Michael and gives him a hug.

"What'd you do then?"

"Well, *obviously*, I gave the guy in the Mercedes head in return for a ride over here. I *had* to. I was worried I was going to be late."

Glances are exchanged. There's some perturbation in the ranks.

"Thank you for that introduction, Michael," Gerry says. "What else do you feel compelled to share with us tonight?"

"Um ... well, first, I don't think of myself as a victim," Michael responds. "I'm a person who has the power to choose my behaviour."

"Absofuckinglutely," someone calls out, but a dozen men who don't really believe in the piety fidget in their seats. Someone swears after burning himself on an errant splash of coffee.

"I do truly believe I was born a suckslut." Michael's breathing has gotten easier, and there's an arrogant edge to the way he carries on. He surveys the room. "I sucked my thumb in the delivery room when there was nothing else to turn to. Teachers and babysitters used to remark on my perseverance. I wore my pacifier to a nubbin. As a child, I could suck the colour off a lollipop. Everlasting gobstoppers lasted me about ten seconds. Popsicles didn't have a chance to melt in my mouth. Chrome off a trailer hitch? You betcha. Every Boy Scout leader this side of the Mississippi wanted me in his den."

Michael bangs the top of the podium with an open palm. Many in the audience jump and look guilty. Others are staring at the movements of Michael's mouth; from the looks on their faces, it's easy to see there's just one thing on their minds.

"On my eighteenth birthday," Michael says, "I sucked off the entire starting lineup of the boys' varsity basketball team—at a single sitting. I spent a summer at the beach doing nothing but inflating rubber rafts; I put the electric air pump to shame."

Michael's face is earnest, his mouth grim. "I am not proud of these things," he says, yet he sounds proud. "But the best I ever had? It was a nineteen-year-old Mormon hoops player, size sixteen shoes. A kid who had never before had his dick sucked. I got him naked in the towel room at a resort where he was playing a tournament. A quick compliment, maybe two, and he was showing me everything the good Lord had given him. Like all young men, his cock was perfectly perpendicular, tight as a tuning fork. And he was so damn proud of it, like a little boy who'd just won the spelling bee. He was eager to show me how his new toy worked.

I swear, the load he shot into me, he'd been saving since puberty."

Michael lowers his head and swallows deeply.

"I know it's wrong," he says. "Not everything is about sucking a stiffy. There's lots of other tremendously important things in life ... ahem ... Like, uh, um. Well, I'm having trouble thinking of any. But there are, I'm sure. It's just that, well, a party without swinging dick—it makes me nervous."

"Amen!" shouts somebody in the circle.

"I'm *soothed* by dick," Michael says. He grips both sides of the lectern. He runs his palms rhythmically up and down the polished edge. He lets his fingertips gently caress and adjust the microphone stem. "Swinging dick in loose trousers—like a metronome counting down the minutes until someone blows a load down my throat. You know what I'm talking about."

There's a murmur of something like assent. Something knowing and brotherly.

"I look at cock in the locker room. I check it out in the shower. I look at it in the urinal. I am the nightmare of every straight man with the Irish curse." He grips both sides of the lectern as if he might vault himself over it. "My experience is that men like to show off their cocks."

This time, there's an audible cheer, but everyone looks as if they're asking themselves: *Is a cheer permitted? Shouldn't we be ashamed of this?*

"You know what I'm talking about!"

Now, there's an unabashed and thoroughly lusty cheer. Michael steps away from the lectern. He paces the room like a maniac. "There are boys who like it up the ass. There are boys who like to watch. Boys who like toys. But me ... my vice? I'm a suckslut. I love cock."

He looks at them defiantly. Is anyone going to dare to stir, to yawn, to express anything but loving approbation?

"It doesn't mean you're a bad person," someone calls out.

"No way!" says someone else. It's a very supportive environment.

Michael's hand burrows deep in his pocket. He squeezes his erection through the cloth.

"Michael," Gerry says. There's a tremor in his voice. "I think we're beginning to get off—off message, I mean."

"What about straight cock?" Michael asks. "I had this buddy back in college. He knew I was a suckslut, but he was cool with it. He said, just keep away from mine. He was hot. He buzzed his hair down to the skull. He always had his eyes squeezed slightly shut as if he was squinting in the sun. This guy enjoyed being looked at. He liked to cause a stir. Stroll buck naked down the hall from the shared showers with his towel over his shoulder. He'd stop and talk and absently play with his cock."

Hidden behind the lectern, Michael pokes the tip of his cock through his open fly. It's thick, pale, and too big for his grip. He brings up his hand, licks his palm, reaches down, and begins to stroke.

"So one day, we were strung out and drinking beers and watching the game in his dorm room. Just the two of us. Sox win, and he changed the channel to *Charlie's Angels*. It was late, but I wasn't about to leave. There was something in the air. I had—have—a fine-tuned instinct for cock. Whenever or wherever it's likely to show its face. My friend peeled off his shirt and threw it at the dirty clothes hamper. He was lying there in just basketball shorts. His hand was beneath the waistband, his eyes on the TV. He yawned and mentioned how horny the Angels made him. All those hot girls. My mouth went dry. I wet my lip with my tongue. There was a rise in my crotch, just as he grabbed his. He had a huge erection; it tented his shorts—like a circus big top. He still wasn't looking at me, but he pulled his basketball shorts down to mid-thigh. I licked down his shaft and pulled at the folds of his loose, fleshy sack. I bobbled the nuts with my tongue. He eased down and put his hand on my shoulder and said, 'Easy. Real slow.' So I licked and lapped and pulled a tube of pina colada-flavoured gel from my pocket. (It was my sixth dick that day; I figured I was due for some dessert.) I squeezed out a dab and worked it into the stiff flesh with my fingers. When I went down again, he went quiet as death. His eyes were still closed. A light scrape of teeth made him tighten and go, 'Mmmmmm.' Sucking his cock was like choking up on the sweetest baseball bat in the world. Drool and lube matted his pubes. I tweaked his nipple with one hand. 'I'm gonna jizz,' he said. I pulled away and milked the shaft, staring at that black eye at the tip, ready to catch the load that squirted free. His belly went tight, abs in stark relief. And then a thick chrism spilled down his shaft like from a slow-flowing volcano. I caught gobs of the stuff in my hands and licked it warm off my fingers. He groaned quietly, and then immediately fell asleep. Man, he tasted so good, it made me want to cut off his shorts and run away with them so I had something to remember him by."

Affirmative grunts rise from the circle of men. Michael's dick throbs. The tip is sticky. The balls are drawn up in his sack. His mouth aches for something hard and fleshy. For a moment, he leaves off stroking.

"Not that I think that's a good thing," he says. His tone suggests the contrary: that it's a very good thing indeed.

"Michael," Gerry warns, "maybe you're not quite ready..."

Michael points at him. On Michael's finger, a flick of pre-cum glints under the dim light. "I know what you're thinking, Gerry: this is too self-aggrandizing. Too much of me in the telling. But I'm the first to admit that I am not in the top ranks of sucksluts. The professionals. The kings."

Michael's accusing finger moves around the circle and comes to rest on a diminutive middle-aged man in a seersucker suit. "My modest friend Matt the Mouth, that's him there. From personal experience I can tell you it doesn't get any better. I bow down before him."

Michael inclines his head.

"Even at his age, he's unerring," says Michael. "A prodigious talent. He can size up a fellow at a hundred yards and rattle off the stats: cut/uncut, length, fast or slow, pubes trimmed or curly, teeth or no teeth, purple head, veiny, crooked—you name it, this guy can feed you the scoops. Some of it experience, but some of it a gift. 'Gotta be good at something,' Matt always says. Unfailingly humble. He always lets you have first choice. And he doesn't mind *sharing* a stray cock now and again. A real saint."

Men crane their heads to get a look at the object of Michael's praise. Michael shakes a knowing finger to temper their spirits.

"But my friends, whether you're Matt, or you're me, or you're you, you know as well as I do—it starts to get you in trouble. Cock will do that. You know how it goes."

"Say it, brother!"

"What was your rock bottom, Michael?" Gerry prompts. "Don't be afraid to share."

"Oh, man. Like when my boss stopped by my desk three days running, and each time I was in the men's room sucking off the new fresh-off-the-boat hottie janitor. Or when my doctor determined that— by volume—my daily diet consists of nine-tenths jizz. Or the fact that my tongue muscle is bigger than my biceps. And no Chap Stick can ever cure my calloused lips."

He opens his mouth for them to see. At the sight of that well-used maw, open and ready for action, a few flies unzip, a kind of Pavlovian reaction, as if Michael's mouth has gravity, capable of drawing cock to him from around the solar system. Sweat breaks out on Gerry's brow. His iron self-control begins to waver.

Michael continues: "Rock bottom? Once, during lesbian party week in P-town, I was so hard-up for cock that I broke into a minivan and stole one poor dyke's entire stock of dildos. Two or three of them in my mouth at a time just to tame the urge." He sighs. "It's a downhill spiral. You swear off the cock. You bottom yourself silly, as if you could so easily exchange your addiction for another orifice. But it always comes back to the swinging dick. The cock at three hundred yards. The hot lawn boy with the big package beneath his Daisy Duke cut-off jeans. The—"

All of a sudden, there's a commotion in the part of the circle farthest from the podium. Michael peers through the haze and smoke. Despite three solid dickless years under his belt, there's Gerry, going at it on his neighbour's manmeat like a kid bobbing for apples at a Halloween party. Michael leaps from behind the lectern. Intent on saving Gerry from his own weakness, he bodily throws himself between Gerry and the object of his affection. Then he sees it: the rigid pole between muscular thighs, the dark pubes against the pale skin, the hip tattoo, and the cock's twitching dance as it searches for Gerry's electric tongue. Who could blame Gerry for falling from the wagon?

Michael kneels. Together, he and Gerry crush their faces into that crotch, licking balls, nibbling the base one on either side. They share it; first Gerry, then Michael, tasting Gerry's saliva slicked all over the cock from head to tip. Gerry rubs the head of it on Michael's parted lips. The pre-cum leaks and tastes of tears.

Another man sees Michael's cock through the open fly of his pants. He bends down and sucks and pulls at the flesh. In turn, another man finds that man's unused member. And on it goes, around the circle, each man helplessly drawn to the next cock over, until the whole meeting dissolves into a massive suckfest, man sucking off man sucking off man, like a chain of fleshy daisies. The proverbial wagon doesn't merely lose a few passengers; it overturns, wrecks, and crashes into a tree. A forest, really. A forest of flesh.

They slink away afterwards, shamefaced, satiated, not a little proud, sneaking quick sniffs of the ass-stink under their fingertips and drying their hands on their pantlegs, backhanding a sleeve across their mouths.

Getting ready, no doubt, for the rest of the dick in the street.

Michael and Gerry look at one another and sigh dejectedly.

"Accept what you cannot change," Michael intones. He glances around at the folding chairs thrown aside, the floor littered with underwear, spent condoms, and gobs of lube.

"Have the courage to change what you can," Gerry answers firmly. The two men pull up their pants and zip their flies and inspect each other's chins for signs of drool.

NEIL SMITH

Extremities

The gloves adored the sensation. Fingers sliding through their cashmere lining, diverging in ten directions, butting against their innermost tips. A sated, exquisite feeling. Heavenly.

The hands trembled. The gloves trembled. Deep inside them, ten fingerprint swirls lit up like the elements of a stove. The juices of the hands, minute droplets of perspiration and skin oils, trickled into the cashmere and were absorbed into the supple, pale pink calfskin of which the gloves were made. This fluid carried with it the secrets of the hands— more secrets than could be revealed by random lines etched on a palm. Instantly the gloves learned the identity of the woman whose hands were the first to burrow inside them. Her name was Dagmar Zavichak. The gloves' first love.

Not one goddamn scratch on me. You try falling fifty thousand fucking feet to the ground and see how you look. Granted, I landed in a rose bush. But, still, roses have thorns, and I'm scratch-free, baby. I am looking mighty fine. Nails clipped and buffed, cuticles tidied, skin smelling of that mint moisturizer slathered on last night. I'm a big foot, man. Size twelve American! I've got little blond hairs on the knuckles of my toes. Blond as the hair on a baby's head—not those rat-ugly black hairs some guys got growing out of their feet. I got me some pumiced heels. I got me some delicate ankles. No shit, I'm size twelve, and I've got the ankles of a ballerina. Ha! I'm tripping out. I'm flying. I'm doing the fucking cancan, man. It's like I'm on speed. Ironic that, because what I don't got, above those delicate ankles of mine, is Captain Robert "Speed" Spedoski.

The calfskin gloves, perched on a pair of mannequin hands atop a glass display case, enjoyed observing their beloved at work. For the past ten years, Dagmar Zavichak had been employed as a loss-prevention agent—

which is to say a store detective—at Winston's, an upscale department store in downtown Chicago. It was her professional duty to appear as inconspicuous as possible, no more substantial, really, than the tissue paper wrapped by a salesclerk around a newly purchased sweater. The gloves believed she rose stupendously to this challenge. To salesclerks who inquired about her unconventional career, she would profess, "I must appear vaporous, a sort of floater in other people's eyes."

To this end, she did not dress in the more ostentatious designer clothing popular in the store, instead favouring Winston's own rather conservative label, Clémence, on which she received a 20 percent discount. In fact, in her decade of employment at Winston's, every item of clothing she had bought there bore the Clémence label. Needless to say, this loyalty to one label worried the gloves, as they were sewn in an Italian house of design known as Giuseppe La Leggia. Yet the gloves were consoled by the fact that each day, as Dagmar Zavichak wandered the store shadowing potential "perps"—the term that loss-prevention agents applied to shoplifters—she would always linger in leather goods and succumb to the urge to try the gloves on.

In calfskin, her hands could move in ways they had never done before. They could make a deft point, beckon gracefully. Gesticulate. In calfskin, they became as eloquent as the hands of baseball umpires, traffic cops, and the deaf. In calfskin, her hands radiated possibility.

Speed's idol, Neil Armstrong, was named after an appendage. Sure, the guy's arm was strong, but it was his right foot—have I mentioned I'm a rightie?—that made that one small step that turned into a giant leap. Our man Speed, ever since he was an eleven-year-old, one gimlet eye trained on a telescope, had dreamed of being the first to set foot on a blood-red world named after the Roman god of war: Mars! But unless Mars has rose bushes, an above-ground pool, a split-level bungalow, a barbecue grill, and a banquet table, you can bet Speed's right nut he never made it.

On Mars, Speed would've weighed a paltry sixty-nine pounds. His day would've lasted forty minutes longer than on Earth. At the equator, he could've basked in a midday temp of seventy degrees. He would've seen gullies, broad plains, mountains higher than Everest, swirling winds called dust devils that whip the soil into red tornadoes. He would've seen two moons in the sky, so tiny he could've jogged around those buggers in an afternoon. I could blab on about Mars, but none of this tells you much about Speed, other than that his lifelong dream was to make a forty-million-mile leap.

That leap was never *my* dream. My name, by the way, is Larry. I have no last name. But, if I did, I'd want a hero's name like Neil Strongarm. Hey, hey, I know, call me Larry Footloose. Ha! My lifelong dream: to be free of Speed.

Mission accomplished.

The gloves looked forward to Mondays, Wednesdays, Fridays, and Sundays, as these were the days Dagmar Zavichak worked at Winston's. On Wednesdays, they became positively giddy with anticipation because between one and two o'clock, her lunch hour, the gloves accompanied the loss-prevention agent into the real world. Why Wednesdays? Because that was the rule. On Wednesdays, Dagmar Zavichak slipped the gloves from the mannequin hands and into her Clémence jacket, deft as the nimblest pickpocket.

The ride in the loss-prevention agent's pocket, as she drifted through women's wear, down the escalator, around endless cosmetic counters and out the revolving front door, was the part of the day's journey the gloves least enjoyed, for they usually shared that dark, intimate pouch with a pair of balled-up mittens whose damp wool and graceless shape the calfskin gloves found particularly disheartening. But today the mittens were not there. The gloves had the roomy pocket to themselves. As their beloved scurried away from Winston's, they fell one against the other in what might be deemed their first attempt at applause.

What went wrong? What happened to the *Zoë X*? Probably something unfathomably stupid brought the bugger down. Remember the *Challenger* back in '86? Disintegrated a minute after liftoff. On the news clips, spectators squinted up with their nonplussed pusses. And that high-school teacher, Christa McAuliffe! Oh God in Heaven, she was my type, that Christa was, with those honest brown eyes, that naturally curly hair. Smart. Good with kids. That tight blue spacesuit zipped halfway down her chest! Not Speed's type, but mine.

Anyway, the *Challenger* rode into the sky on the back of a huge blimp-shaped fuel tank, like a remora on a shark. Also attached to that tank were two rocket boosters to provide thrust. The joints of those boosters were sealed with what you call O-rings. Picture the rubber washers in your faucet, only bigger. Well, it was 32 degrees Fahrenheit the morning of the *Challenger* launch, and so the rubber O-rings were too cold to expand and seal the joints. Hot gases and flames shot out of the booster causing the whole kit-and-caboodle to blow. Where's the justice, man: Christa was done in by a fucking washer.

How thrillingly loud was the world outside Winston's easy-listening cocoon. Hare Krishnas shook tambourines. A skateboarder cursed at a taxi. Pedestrians shouted into cellphones. An ambulance dopplered by. After indolent days atop their display case, the gloves were elated to be on the move, to be filled with hands whose fingertips exuded the pungent smell of aged cheddar from the sandwich Dagmar Zavichak had hastily eaten before fetching the gloves.

Where would their beloved take them today? In their outings thus far, the gloves had travelled to the Art Institute of Chicago, a bookshop, and a supermarket, and each time they learned something new about the loss-prevention agent, something alluding to a pattern as persistent as the black-eyed Susans running the length of her silk scarf. At the art museum, they learned that her favourite artist was Paul Klee, for she looked only at his paintings, not once glancing sideways to view, say, a Kandinsky. At the bookshop, she riffled only through the works of the novelist John Irving. At the supermarket, the gloves handled prickly pears and a pineapple. What bliss! But any canned or boxed food they placed in her basket sported the exact same label so that at the checkout counter the cashier exclaimed, "You sure like Consumer's Choice!" Dagmar Zavichak, the gloves' beloved, replied, "I'm a very loyal shopper."

Okay, okay, you want to hear about Speed. Everybody always wants the nitty-gritty on Robert Spedoski. Now that he's the new Icarus, they'll no doubt want even more. You want to hear why him and me didn't see eye to eye. To put it simple: Speed wasn't up to snuff. Speed didn't have *The Right Snuff*. Ha! You hear about transsexuals being born in the wrong bodies. Men who don't want their pricks. Well, I was born in the wrong body, too. He was a prick, and I didn't want him.

No, but maybe I'm being too hard on Speed. Give the guy a break, Larry. Cut him some slack. He treated you okay. For crying out loud, he massaged your tootsies with mint moisturizer he forked out twenty bucks for. Where would you be without him? I'll tell you where: right here, in a rose bush in a suburban backyard where some bald dude in a suit is carrying a bowl of fruit punch across his lawn.

One calfskin glove gripped the man's hand and released. As it did so, the man's lifeline and other traces of his touch faded from the glove's palm like a child's drawings in the sand, washed away by the surf. The gloves could not know this man the way they knew Dagmar Zavichak. She was their beloved; he was merely a fleeting encounter in a coffee shop.

For this outing, this blind date, the gloves enjoyed a perfect view of the proceedings: they sat decorously on the table, ten digits entwined. They glowed pink and throbbed like a calf's excised heart. "The usual?" asked the waitress. Their beloved answered, "Naturally." For his part, the man requested orange pekoe tea, and the gloves knew that Dagmar Zavichak admired how he delivered his order forcefully, as if no other tea leaf would do. This outing looked promising at first. But later, as the man talked about himself and the mutual funds he sold, he spilled three drops of his orange pekoe and neglected to mop them up, he scattered granules of sugar on his placemat and inadvertently crunched them with his elbows, and, for no apparent reason, he inserted a finger into his ear and shook the digit vigorously. Such behaviour would not do.

Consequently, Dagmar Zavichak grew restless, as did the gloves. They fidgeted. They tucked a lock of hair behind her ear. They plucked a loose eyelash from her cheek. They raised her bowl of café au lait to her lips so she could gulp the warm froth. Soon one glove was leaping in front of her face to expose the wristwatch just below its cuff. "Time flies," their beloved said. The date freeze-dried a smile. He was not, the gloves knew, Mr. Klee or Mr. Irving. There were so many ways a man could fail, and this man had. He did not merit her devotion.

As far as I'm concerned, shoes got soles but they got no soul. That expression "walking in someone else's shoes" should be "someone else's feet." You wanna walk in Speed's feet. Well, Larry's an obliging fellow. Larry'll let ya.

Okay, this is going back five years. NASA has announced how many greenbacks your jaunt to the red planet is gonna gobble up and you're miffed because the media is moaning the money should go into a more worthy cause. Channel it into Fruit Loops so no American kiddie goes to school with a gurgling tummy. Funnel it into defense against those godless nations beheading our citizens live on the web. Still, people love you, and NASA knows it. You can run a five-minute mile. You've got a black belt in karate. You're eloquent. Just listen to yourself talk to an auditorium full of students at Carnegie Mellon University. You liken the *Zoë X* mission to a certain journey launched in 1492 by Mr. Cristoforo Colombo. Each young man in the room is King Ferdinand, each young woman Queen Isabella. And they're buying what you're selling, namely that finding primitive, methane-farting microbes far beneath the Martian surface is vital to their VIP-DVD-SUV existences on Earth. You explain that life sprouted on the young Mars and may still linger underground. "Life tries to hang on," you tell the students. "Life does everything it can to survive."

Later, walking to your hotel, you cut through an alleyway and there's this pie-eyed bum sitting on a smashed microwave oven, some down-and-out who smells like a bag of rotting onions. He scrambles up, blocks your path, throws you a goofy smile. His nose is scabby and sunburnt. In your head, an editorial hollers: *Funnel the money into housing for the homeless!* "Spare some—" the bum gets out before your right foot—old Larry himself, dressed in a soulless loafer—connects with the guy's mouth. The bum pitches backwards and crashes down. Blood dribbles from his split lip. Is he dead? You stand over him. No, he's still breathing. You say, "Sometimes life hangs on too long."

Of course, Dagmar Zavichak was not the only woman to slip her hands deep into the calfskin gloves. Yet no other woman lingered inside their bowels; no other handprints burned into their skin. Stuffed with the lardy hands of these other women, the gloves felt like a trollop; filled with Dagmar Zavichak's slender hands, they felt like a pampered mistress dined at a fashionable restaurant while the wife, the pair of oblivious wool mittens, remained sequestered at home. For the gloves' next outing, Dagmar Zavichak took them to lunch at Chez Julien, where they fingered satisfyingly heavy silverware and a linen napkin still warm from the dryer.

As a special surprise, she ordered the veal cutlet and kept her hands gloved throughout her meal. She pricked the morsels of meat with her fork, brought them to her lips and slowly chewed the veal to a paste. As she swallowed, the calfskin gloves quivered, for now Dagmar Zavichak was inside of them and they were, in a way, inside of her.

Yet when the meal came to an end, their beloved returned them once again to their post on the display case at Winston's. How they yearned to be hers alone. Would their beloved ever take them home? They dreamed of this home, this mitten-less home with prints by Mr. Klee on the walls, novels by Mr. Irving on the bookshelves, Consumer's Choice canned goods in the cupboards. Beneath the quiet equanimity, the simmering obsessions.

My cover's blown! Mr. Suburbia, the bald dude in the suit, is squatting in front of my rose bush, and two guesses who he comes face to foot with. Well, he freaks. His face contorts like a cartoon: eyes bugging, mouth gaping, nostrils flared. He grunts, falls backwards, drops his clippers and the roses he's cut. I'm thinking he's having a fucking heart attack—he's a pudgy older dude, a bit jowly, grey beard—but, no, he springs back up and moves in close, parting the leaves of the bush with his hands. "Jesus H. Christ," he mutters. Then the guy starts combing the backyard, foraging through the hedges, peering into the swimming pool. He's looking for other parts! What does he expect to find? A kneecap behind the compost bin, an elbow on the roof of the shed, Speed's right nut under the barbecue? It's like he's Isis, the Egyptian goddess, looking for pieces of her dismembered husband Osiris. That's a good one: our golden boy, Robert Spedoski, as god of the underworld.

They were the first male hands to penetrate the gloves. Small and moist, they slid in easily. As ten fingers flexed like boys in gym class doing deep knee bends, ten fingerprints burned into the gloves' tips; if the calfskin still had hair, that hair would have been bristling. Something was amiss. These hands were jumpy, kinetic, and the perspiration seeping into the cashmere lining could have curdled milk. At the other end of the appendages was a man whose thin moustache appeared pencilled on. His eyes had bulbous whites and pinprick pupils. The gloves recalled a watercolour at the art museum; *Face in Hand* was the painting, a self-portrait of Mr. Klee resting his head in his palm. Yet this man was not gentle Mr. Klee. This man, the gloves realized, was a bandit. This man was a perp.

A wedding reception, man. A goddamn wedding reception. People mill around the yard, schmooze and guffaw. Wine glasses tinkle. Little kids weave in and out of everybody's legs in a squealing game of tag. People wolf down calzones brought in from the restaurant owned by the father-of-the-bride, pudgy Mr. Suburbia. Minutes after he discovered yours truly, his guests started swarming into his backyard. He barely had time to drag the barbecue in front of my rose bush. But I can see under the belly of the thing. Larry's got a good view.

Guess what. Fuck me if one of the guests isn't a dead ringer for the dead astronautess Christa McAuliffe. Same honest face, same curly hair. Dressed in pale pink, she is—dress, shoes, and gloves. She and the bride are standing away from the crowd, not far from my bush, and Christa is talking about Speed. "So close to his dream he could almost lick the ice crystals on Mars," she says. "Imagine spending every breath of your life longing for something you'll never have." Her voice sounds sad. Don't be sad, Christa. The lanky bride, in her silver sheath of a dress, looks like a rocket booster. She says Christa is being a gloomy Gus on her special day. She says she's got her dream: the giddy groom doing cartwheels under the clothesline to entertain the kiddies. Then the father-of-the-bride butts in. "Come away from there," he says, glancing at my rose bush. "Come join the living."

Soon everybody's dancing. Man, I'd like to trip the light fantastic myself. A cancan, man, but no can do. My dream's come true, but without Speed, I ain't the twinkletoes I used to be.

While the perp stood at the urinal, the calfskin gloves, appalled and frightened by the turn of events, attempted to lose themselves in memories of happier times. As the stinking stream of urine sizzled against porcelain, the gloves drifted back to their childhood in a factory in Florence. The good heady smell of leather. The lilting voices of sewing machines in song. The needle gently puncturing the skin. Gloves in a spectrum of colours lying together like litters of kittens. Each finger on each glove one possible direction in which their life might point them.

The calfskin gloves had not dreamed that this would be their fate: shaking the last dribbly drops out of a thick, dim-witted digit devoid of nail, knuckle, fingerprint. The gloves shoved this flesh back into the perp's pants, raised his zipper, and, in front of the restroom mirror, combed themselves through his hair. They shuddered at the sight of his face, as milky white as cooked veal. Away from the mirror, they pushed open the door, and there, standing in the little hallway, was their saviour. Beloved! Oh, such sweet, sweet relief.

"Sir, we do not allow customers to bring merchandise into the restrooms." Her voice wavered. "Oh, so sorry," said the perp. One gloved thumb pressed the button on a drinking fountain as the perp bent over and slurped. When he stood, Dagmar Zavichak was still there. "May I have the gloves?" she said, her voice more forceful. "Yes, yes, of course," he said. He made a movement as if to strip the gloves off, but then his arms shot up and sank ten fingers into the meat of Dagmar Zavichak's neck.

I haven't mentioned Marty, have I? Marty was my partner. Marty was a leftie, and like most lefties he was a bit slow on the uptake. But loyal. God, Marty was as loyal as a golden goddamn retriever. You want proof: his name was originally Lionel, but he changed it to Marty when Speed started obsessing over the red planet. I said to him, "Why not Marsy, you plantar wart?" And he said, "Oh, Larry, Marsy ain't a name."

Still, Marty was a good guy. He'd scratch my back, I'd scratch his. But he never really understood Speed. Not like I did. For instance, not one family dinner went by when Speed didn't curse his dad, badmouth his mom, and toot his own horn to his brothers, but Marty would make excuses. "It ain't easy being a hero to the nation, Larry," he'd say. Or he'd change the topic: "Remember when Speed was eleven and took us roller-skating for the first time? Remember how clumsy we all were? Even you were laughing, Larry. Even stick-in-the-mud you. You said it was like trying to walk on the frigging moon, excuse my French."

Marty was a nostalgic bugger. Poor good-natured Marty. Wonder if he felt it. Felt what I did as the Zoë X lifted its gargantuan ass off the tarmac and blasted toward the heavens. Speed never shared much with me and Marty. We were too far from his brain, too far from his heart. But in those final moments, I felt something course through his veins, something as clean and fortifying as milk. A mix of resignation and serenity.

That's when I knew.

I knew what Speed had already realized: that the Zoë X would blow. He knew there were hiccups in its design, something obviously harder to fix than an idiotic O-ring, but he never pointed out the glitches for fear of having the project shelved for good. Speed couldn't wait any longer. All his life he'd wanted to be millions of miles away from the rest of humanity. He couldn't wait a fucking day longer. "Goodbye, Marty," I said as the cabin disintegrated.

The gloves had never been closer to their beloved. Dagmar Zavichak had sunk her flesh into them, but never had they sunk their flesh into her. Through the strings of muscle in her neck, the buttery-soft gloves could feel her heart beating, beating, beating, pounding, pounding. From her mouth came the bleating of a caged, motherless calf. Her lovely hands tried prying the gloves off, but the gloves were reluctant to break their warm embrace. Up to the perp's face, her hands rose. They scratched his cheeks. They poked his eyes. Only then did the calfskin gloves release their grip.

Oh, but what had they done? What had the gloves done? The shame! The pink of their leather surely deepened from such grievous shame. Yet the gloves had no chance to apologize to their beloved, now slumped against the wall and clutching at her own throat, because the perp scuttled off and then broke into a run, his arms pumping, the gloves slapping past racks of clothing, knocking a wide-brimmed flying saucer of a hat off a woman's head. Out the revolving door they pushed, their lining drenched from the perp's spongy palms.

In the spring morning, a tribe of Hare Krishnas waved their tambourines. The perp jounced their robes as he shot by, pulling at the calfskin as if it were scorching his hands. He peeled the gloves off and, frantic, pushed them through the swinging lid of a street-side recycling bin where they landed crumpled atop a heap of soda cans tacky from spilt orangeade.

Lying there in the dark, their cuffs turned inside out, they told themselves they deserved this fate. They had betrayed their beloved. They had grown so attached to Dagmar Zavichak that they had wanted to be permanently attached to her. Like an appendage. Like a hand. Like that hand now snaking through the lid of the recycling bin, its familiar Y-shaped lifeline a divining rod. "Here we are!" the gloves called out. "Oh, sweet Jesus, here we are!"

It's midnight. The party's over; everybody's gone home. Crickets play a concert, their wings their violins. A neighbour's revolving sprinkler whizzes and tweets. Tonight the sky's cloudless. Look due south fifty degrees above the horizon and you'll spot a red star. Guess who?

The door at the back of the house clacks open. The porch light clicks on. Two figures walk across the yard, one holding a flashlight whose beam homes in on a yard swing. "I'm sure my gloves are here somewhere, Mr. DiMaria," a voice says. A voice I recognize from the party. The voice of Christa McAuliffe. "Oh sweet Jesus," I call out. "I'm over here!"

Snug inside her pocket, the gloves could hear Dagmar Zavichak's co-workers cooing with concern. Your throat, one woman said, will surely bruise. The police, one man said, must be called in. He got away, their beloved repeated. He got away with a pair of calfskin gloves! Such mayhem over a pair of gloves, said another man. Oh, but they're lost, their beloved exclaimed. They're gone! Inside her pocket, the gloves were happy: they were going home.

It's 2 AM. For light, we've got a big communion wafer of a moon and a flashlight lying on the ground not far from my bush. Mr. Suburbia— Mr. DiMaria—is over by the shed where he's been shovelling for the past fifteen minutes. His backyard is where Speed took his final step for man, and Mr. DiMaria doesn't want that kind of notoriety. After digging his hole, he leans his shovel against the shed, wipes his brow, and picks up a cardboard box. As he comes for me, I recognize the box for what it is. A shoebox. Fitting.

He sets it down and scoots the barbecue aside. From the barbecue hang what look like hot-dog tongs. He uses them. He parts the leaves and branches and those goddamn metal claws drag me out by the toes. He drops me into the box, muttering, "I'm sorry, Speed." I want to say, "The name's Larry," but instead I think the same thing: I'm sorry, Speed. Sorry that in the days counting down to your big countdown I kept hoping you'd fail big time.

The gloves' presence in their beloved's home had ramifications. A ripple effect. Out with the old—out with Mr. Klee, Mr. Irving, the Clémence clothing, the Consumer's Choice—and in with the new. New outfits to be hung in the closet, a new artist to be selected for the walls, new novels to be read, new food to be sampled. Such a hullabaloo that their beloved grew cranky and eventually quite ill.

One day, after a sobbing breakdown during which she tore to bits her new Roy Lichtenstein poster, *Study of Hands*, Dagmar Zavichak changed everything back. The old—the familiar, soothing old—returned. Oh hello again, Mr. Irving and Mr. Klee. Welcome home! As for the calfskin gloves, they were thrust into the farthest reaches of her closet. There they waited, fearful of their own waning love. There were so many ways a pair of gloves could fail, and these gloves had, hadn't they? Yet they remained hopeful, knowing one day they would again be brought out into the world. At Winston's, their outings were restricted to Wednesdays. Why Wednesdays? Because that was the rule. In Dagmar Zavichak's home, the new rule was this: she could wear her pink gloves exclusively to events out of state. For instance, the wedding of her friend Theresa down in Florida.

Mr. DiMaria retrieves his flashlight and bends over the shoebox to examine me up close. My gorgeousness. But he goes wobbly-kneed and bumps against the barbecue—and down flutter two wings, two pink angels that alight on my hide. The gloves Christa had come back for and never found. "If I find them, I'll mail them to you," Mr. DiMaria had promised. "They're nothing special," Christa had replied. "Give them to charity." And he will. He'll give them to me, a guy with one foot in the grave. Christa's hands to caress me, tickle my sole. Hands to hold me forever. What a gift, man. Like they say about donated organs: the gift of a lifetime.

On a wedding day in Florida, the gloves tasted the fluids of Dagmar Zavichak's body. In a hotel room, they pasted a pincurl to her forehead with the saliva from her mouth. In a church, they rubbed away tears as the priest declared "till death do you part." In a parking lot, they wiped her runny nose as the Florida flora coughed up its pollen. In a bathroom at the father-of-the-bride's home, they slid a tissue between her legs and absorbed a drop of urine. Yet these fluids carried no secrets. Urine, mucous, saliva, tears, sweat—they were no more evocative than the flat ginger ale Dagmar Zavichak was sipping at the backyard reception. As she sliced herself some wedding cake, the gloves half-hoped she would plunge the knife into her wrist. Blood! Perhaps only blood could rekindle the love, the extreme love, that she and the gloves had once shared.

It came as no surprise to the gloves when Dagmar Zavichak mislaid them atop a barbecue grill. From their perch, they watched the celebrations, the hot sun bleaching their skin. They studied the people gathered there. Among these guests was perhaps a new beloved, for earlier in the day, as Theresa Fritz, née DiMaria, squealed on the church steps, the gloves had leapt into the air to pluck the bouquet of flowers from the sky.

On their cardboard roof comes the pitter-patter not of rain but of earth. Falling earth. In their bed, they intertwine. Beloved and beloved and beloved. Fingers stroke. Toes wriggle. A heel grinds. The sole sweats on a palm. A glove stretches open its calfskin cuff, and the foot thrusts in, the toe print of the big toe as enormous and electrifying as a whirlpool galaxy. Their love is obsessive. Yet they take their time. There is no rush: they have the rest of their lives. They are brides and groom, and this is their wedding night.

Tess Fragoulis

Words to Flesh

It was a regular sort of event. Some plastic chairs were set up in a haphazard semi-circle, encouraging an intimacy that would probably not be achieved since almost all of them were empty. The few that were filled were occupied by a handful of faithful friends, three or four bookstore employees who were momentarily excused from their duties, and at least one person who was insane. No reading was complete without a smiling lunatic who had wandered in out of the cold, attracted by the store's bright lights and narrow corridors of bookshelves behind which he could hide and whisper in code to unsuspecting shoppers. The employees—the audience on the payroll—were also easy to pick out. Most were pimply-faced youths in their early twenties who had obviously spent more time with books than people; they smiled at her shyly before moving awkwardly to their seats. The other type was the overweight, bearded hippie who after years of indifference and ennui had risen to the position of manager. She liked the crazy people better. Like children they sat and stared at her unselfconsciously, laughing out loud and clapping when something in the story excited them. Most people who attended readings were an over-serious lot, as afraid to titter as to fart in public lest they draw disdainful attention to themselves. As they sat there, waiting for her to begin, they already looked somewhat guilty.

She heard the final cattle-call for her reading over the bookstore's public address system, "Attention all shoppers..." These desperate and monotonous announcements always made her feel like a crate of bruised tomatoes in the produce aisle, though the tomatoes probably got a better crowd. It was hard to get a decent tomato in the city, whereas you couldn't swing a dead cat without hitting a published writer these days. A few nearby browsers glanced over at her standing by the podium, and then scurried off in the opposite direction and down the stairs. Only one of the itinerant shoppers—a tall, dark, and handsome-enough stranger—

slipped into a seat in the third row, slightly to the left of the podium. She looked at him for a moment, took him in. She thought she recognized him but couldn't quite place him, so she decided he was just a variation on one of the seven faces she believed existed in the world, whose owners confused her in foreign cities by evoking people she knew. He, however, stared at her with the confidence of a man who has already been kissed, and when he winked at her she quickly turned her attention to her book, riffling through the pages as if she were just at that moment deciding what she was going to read to this shipwreck of an audience.

The evening's host, a short skinny man with a big nose, was trying to muster enough enthusiasm to make up for the empty seats. He got all his facts wrong when he introduced her, but she just smiled and nodded and didn't bother correcting him. What for? When she became famous she wouldn't have to bother creating her own myths. The handsome-enough man leaned forward with his elbows on his knees, his chin in his open palms, and watched her intensely as she began to read. The crazy person also stared intensely and smiled brightly, and the combination of their two gazes, for some reason, cheered her up. So instead of rushing through her story as she'd intended, she found herself slowing down as she reached the midway point, offering every sentence, then every word, like a shiny lure.

After it was over, the handsome-enough man approached her at the signing. Truth be told, he was only barely handsome, but, given the slim pickings on the reading circuit in general and in the bookstore that evening in particular, he fulfilled the role of best-of-the-worst, and focusing upon him had made time pass just a little bit more pleasantly. He handed her a copy of her book and a fountain pen, but when she asked for his name he replied, "Make me up."

She signed it *to the mystery man.*

He remained a mystery even after they started sleeping together. He gave her his phone number but wouldn't tell her where he lived. At first she imagined he was married, but, since he placed no limitations on the hours she could call him and slept over at her apartment a few nights every week with no apparent anxiousness to leave after the deed was done, she concluded that his apartment was a bachelor cave with no toilet seat and a mattress on the floor, and she was happy to avoid that type of show of affection at such an early stage in their relationship. She was quite satisfied spending all their time together at her apartment, where everything was warm and pretty, where her sheets were clean and she was surrounded by all her things, by all her books. He didn't seem to mind either. In the comfort of her queen-sized bed, they read passages from her favourite novels to each other, taking turns choosing which one to share. He often chose one of the books she had written when it was his turn, and though she suspected this might be a simple and obvious form of flattery, hearing his deep voice speak her words made her ravenous. After a while he could recite whole passages from several different stories, standing naked and glorious in the centre of the bed, or curled up behind her like a shell, whispering in her ear. Sometimes she forgot the passages were her own compositions and was convinced that one of her imaginings had come to life, speaking to her in a language she longed to hear and performing acts she dared not utter out loud. She had never been so taken, so happy. She stopped inquiring about his home life and waited for him every other night to press more of her words into her flesh.

What he did for a living was also somewhat vague. He called himself an entrepreneur, a freelancer, and a self-made man. But the nature of his enterprise and how he'd made himself and his money was not entirely clear. That he had money was certain. There was never a question about who would pay for dinner when they went out; elaborate arrangements of exotic flowers arrived at her door regularly, signed from characters in her stories; and she only had to mention a passing interest in a book for it to appear on her bedside table. If she said she'd been thinking about the paintings of Max Ernst, by his next visit an expensive, hardcover edition of the painter's collected works would be sitting there in its original wrap. If she expressed an interest in Japanese cuisine, an elaborate three-volume set of authentic recipes would materialize. And any author—dead, alive, famous, obscure—whose name she happened to drop in a conversation would find his or her way into the bedroom before the lights went out. She figured he smuggled them in while she was brushing her teeth and dusting herself with honey-flavoured powder that made her skin shimmer in the candlelight. It was a perpetual surprise party between the sheets, since she never quite knew who would be coming to bed with them on any given night. Not only did this variety whet their passion, the Japanese cookbooks were as much of a lubricant as the nonsensical analyses of modern art. In a pinch, even a well-chosen word from the dictionary could get them going, their sex smooth and lyrical as a well-wrought and complex sentence.

There was another thing she noticed as the books piled up next to her side of the bed. With every addition to her library he would change slightly. With the arrival of the Japanese three-volume set came a floor-length, embroidered red kimono. This was not an additional gift for her, but a costume for him, and when he was done impersonating the Shogun Chef he crawled under the covers without taking it off. After they'd made love, she ran her fingers over imprints of cherry blossoms and nightingales that the threads had left on her skin. But it was not just the costumes—she liked the costumes—something deeper changed within him: the texture and the colour of his skin, the slant of his eyes, which she only had to take one look into to realize she was now in bed with a complete stranger. This was not entirely without its charms. With the Max Ernst edition, it was his accent that changed, an almost imperceptible clipping of the ends of words, a harshness at the beginnings, and each syllable was released with the sharpness and speed of a stream of bullets that left holes in the headboard. When she asked him to stop, to speak in his normal voice, he pretended not to know what she was talking about, planted his lips onto hers with a brusqueness that was unusual, and pushed the art book onto the floor.

Though she loved the books he brought her and the novelty of the games they inspired, she was much happier when he read her own stories and became one of the men she had already imagined and desired. She piled all of the books he'd brought her into a box and hid them in the closet, then began writing a series of stories for the sole purpose of turning him into the man she believed he could be, the man she thought she wanted. She fanned these manuscripts out on his nightstand and lay back, waiting. He was, as always, more than happy to oblige, and things between them proceeded in this manner for quite a while.

Life outside the bedroom and the pages of her stories also proceeded, but without her. She received invitations to book launches and to other people's readings, but did not go. When her agent called to inquire how her new book was coming along, she replied, "Well, very well," though the truth was much more complicated. There was no new book because since he'd arrived she'd felt no need to write anything but the scenarios they could play out. Any other work seemed trite and pointless, for the enjoyment of everyone but herself. Occasionally envelopes would arrive containing newspaper clippings and letters in which people she didn't know said things about her work that she didn't understand, so she stopped reading her mail. When her last book was nominated for a small literary prize, the bookstore where she'd met him all those months ago (all those books ago) sent a basket of fruit with a singing stripper, who invited her to read again. She had not been back there since the night her mystery man had asked her to make him up. She had no use for bookstores anymore; he provided everything she needed, and all of her literature was created and consumed in-house. But she graciously accepted the bookstore's invitation, picturing him sitting in the audience again, no longer a stranger, listening to her read then ducking with her into the poetry aisle to make love while the crazies watched from behind the shelves. She wrote this out for him, as she did all her requests. She wrote it in the form of a short story that detailed their first meeting, their history up until then, ending with the part about the poetry aisle, but adding ellipses so he would understand that there was another sentence, paragraph, chapter that was not yet written in their ongoing tale. The night before the reading, she placed this story on his bedside table after he'd fallen asleep, and when she woke up in the morning both he and the few sheets of paper were gone.

She prepared herself for the reading with an eagerness she had never felt before. She no longer cared about who would or wouldn't show up since her lover would be there—her perfect audience of one, the other half whom she'd been writing for and to all these years. She put on the deep blue dress that was his favourite and at the last moment decided underwear would not be required. She arrived at the bookstore a little bit earlier than necessary to scope out the best corner for the act her reading would merely be a preamble to. Getting caught didn't worry her; in fact, it would only enhance her reputation. Her readers liked to believe she was what she wrote, and for once she was willing to oblige.

The evening's host, the same short skinny man with the big nose, spotted her and walked over to welcome her and congratulate her on the nomination with the same false kindness found in Jehovah's Witnesses until you slam the door. She shook his hand and allowed him to guide her toward the podium. She scanned the small audience for her leading man, the other half of her story, but he was not there yet. No matter, she thought. He had never disappointed her, had never refused to participate. But as the time approached for her to begin regaling the handful of employees, the two or three crazies, and the few shoppers looking for bargain tomatoes, she began to sense that he was not going to show up, and her naked buttocks, barely concealed under the short blue dress, blushed.

It was on her way out of the bookstore, her steps heavy and disappointed, her eyes brimming with tears, and her hands pulling down the hem of her dress, that she noticed the posters on the wall behind the row of cash registers. A police lineup where he was every suspect. She read the words *Reward* and *Book Thief* but did not immediately understand what they meant. What she understood better were the sketches: one of him with the face of the red-kimonoed shogun, one with sunken cheeks and shadows etched under his piercing blue eyes, and three others where he looked like the men in her stories—two of them published, one not. She ran out of the store, ran all the way home wondering what to get rid of—the box of books or him? She wasn't sure what would be worse.

She found him sitting on her bed surrounded by all the books he'd brought her, all the stories she'd written for him, and he was almost unrecognizable from one second to the next as the expressions of a thousand men flitted across his face. She stared at him, speechless, trying to focus on one single feature that she knew and loved, but even when he began to speak in what she imagined was the same voice she'd heard on the first night they'd met, she was not sure who he was. He made no excuses. What came out of his mouth in that voice she did not know was a diatribe, a speech prepared and rehearsed a thousand times with this very moment in mind.

There was no difference between them, he began. He loved books as much as she did if not more; he was obsessed with them and could never satisfy his lust, his hunger for them. He ate books for breakfast, lunch, and dinner, and still there were not enough stories to satisfy his need. "You are what you eat, and we all need to eat to survive," he stated as if ending a paragraph, then took a deep breath and continued.

It was because of her that he existed at all. Without writers there could be no books; without books, no book thieves. He was created by her in the same way she created her characters, but she could not expect to control all aspects of her creations once she loosed them upon the world. It was simple and obvious enough for him to become the perfect lover because she imagined it: the teenage boy who watched through her bathroom window as she washed her face or the tortured artist with the strong and wicked hands. But there was a dark side to her imagination, darker than even she knew or was willing to admit. And it was in this place that the book thief was born along with her desire for him—not for the man who would steal her published works from the shelves of the local store, but for the one who would take the books she had not yet published or written, the stories huddling inside her like a litter of blind fetuses, as well as those that had not yet been conceived. Was that not what every writer ultimately wanted? To be freed of her stories no matter how it was done, to have someone willing to take them off her hands, to bring them to life outside of her? All these years as she scribbled in solitude wasn't she really just waiting for someone to steal her soul?

His self-righteousness spent, he collapsed onto the pillows and began to cry. She stood back, rooted to the spot, unable or unwilling to go to him, to comfort him. She watched him with a clinical eye and tried out words like "desperate," "unrepentant," and "maudlin," admitting to herself that this was not necessarily the chapter she expected to follow the sex in the poetry aisle, but one could never be too rigid about these things. She did not wonder whether what he had said was true. Some of it struck her as plausible. She did know that desperate need to take in and to spit out words, sentences. And despite what he had assumed, she did have an inner book thief, and not as far down in the shadows as she would have liked. Once, when she was a poor student, she had stolen a book of African tales because she did not have the money to buy it, and it had seemed like the greatest injustice in the universe that she should be deprived of its magic. She'd needed that book with the urgency of a pee after a long car ride, and stealing it, slipping it into her school bag, provided the same sense of release and transgression as squatting on the side of the highway while cars whizzed by—some noticing her, others oblivious to her breach of manners. She still cherished that book, relished the criminal thrill of acquisition. But she had not made a career out of stealing books as he had. She had chosen the other route. She stole lives instead.

When his quiet sobbing subsided, she spoke. "Did you steal my book?" she asked in a voice she did not recognize as her own. It was the voice of some character who had a solid moral stance.

"Yes," was his almost inaudible reply. He had gone to the reading with the sole intention of stealing it right under her nose. But the high had been far more intense than he'd expected. It was as if he had kidnapped her, then fallen in love with his victim and victimizer.

At that point she decided to do what she always did when faced with a quandary. She pulled out her notebook, sat on the floor, and began to write about him lying there on her bed, surrounded by the purloined books he had given her along with himself, struggling with his feeling, and trying to tell her things she should have already guessed, that she knew without knowing, that she'd been reluctant to admit. She described him as a handsome-enough man with a quiet voice who loved books so much that he devoured them like salted peanuts. And as she wrote she began to recognize him again. He took shape as that lover hidden behind all the others, lurking faceless in dark corners, in the empty spaces between books on a shelf, waiting to pounce, to ravish, to relieve her of the only thing she had to give.

Dressing Up

Peter stands in front of the mirror, looking at his face.

He isn't a ten, he knows that, but he's at least an eight. Blue eyes and dark hair with a pale complexion, the dark shadow of his beard making him unmistakably male.

He doesn't pluck his eyebrows or wear makeup. He's never exfoliated or masked or done anything more with his face than wash it with soap and water. He is a guy after all. A man. Male through and through.

Ben comes and stands behind him, head on his shoulder, body fitting snugly against him. One of those big hands comes around and slide along his belly, stroking, hot through the silk of Peter's dress as Ben's cheek rubs his own.

"I like this one," Ben says softly.

"Yeah?" Peter reaches up and puts his arms around Ben's shoulders, the movement pushing his hips out, his hardening cock unmistakable beneath the clinging blue silk.

"Yeah."

"What do you like about it? The colour? The texture? The way it falls over my body?"

"You. I like the you part of it."

Peter laughs softly. "So you'd be just as happy if I was naked. Or wearing shorts and a T-shirt."

"No, I didn't say that."

"It's true, though."

"No, I..." Ben puts a kiss on his neck and moves slowly around him, eyes watching him in the mirror, fingers sliding over him. When Ben faces him, gazing at Peter now and not at the apparition in the mirror, Ben goes slowly to his knees.

Peter's lids grow heavy, and he groans softly, fingers trailing over Ben's face, over the sunshine curls and the tanned skin. Ben turns to nuzzle his hands, lips warm, tongue hot, wet as it flicks out to tease over the pads of his fingers. Ben takes one finger into his mouth, sucking gently, tugging on Peter's flesh.

He can feel each pull of Ben's mouth in his cock, and he moans, his flesh swelling, pushing at the silk. God, that feels good, the soft, cool silk and the hint of Ben's warmth beyond it.

Ben lets Peter's finger go with a pop, grinning up at him. Wicked, beautiful man.

Whimpering now, Peter shifts his hips, pushing his cock against the heat of Ben's face.

"Wanton," Ben accuses, making Peter laugh, a shiver of delight going up his spine.

"Turn just a bit," Ben orders, shifting himself, hands landing on Peter's hips to encourage him to move.

Peter does, his body suddenly in profile in the mirror, both of them looking, watching in the mirror as Ben's mouth opens and wraps around the tip of Peter's cock, quickly soaking the silk.

A choked noise comes from Peter's throat, a shudder moving through him. He doesn't know which is better, the way it looks or the way it feels; then Ben takes a little more in and sucks harder, and Peter knows he's fooling himself: nothing can look as good as this feels.

Ben finds Peter's slit through the silk; with that pointed tongue, he plays with it, dragging a groan from Peter. Ben's grin is downright evil now. "You like that?" And that lovely, hot tongue is licking Ben's lips, which are no longer wrapped around Peter's cock.

"Tease." The word falls from Peter's mouth onto Ben and makes those blue eyes twinkle.

"I'm not the one in the dress that clings to every angle."

"It turns you on," Peter breathes, watching the blush race up Ben's face. "You're hard, and not from the sucking."

"Not *just* from the sucking," Ben corrects.

"So you wouldn't prefer me in shorts and a T-shirt."

"I like you as you are," Ben admits.

"How about naked?"

Ben's blush gets darker, the heat beneath Peter's wandering fingertips increasing. "I want you in the dress, Peter. In this dress."

It's everything he's ever wanted to hear, and yet it seems so unreal, that Ben is on his knees in front of him, saying it, wanting him in this dress. It wasn't always like this...

They were on drink number three before Ben worked up the courage to ask about the dress. Peter had been waiting patiently, watching Ben skirt around the topic until the alcohol kicked in.

"Are you a drag queen?"

Peter shook his head. "No."

"Transgendered?"

Peter laughed softly. *They always want to know. They always need their labels, and it bothers them when they can't pigeonhole me.* It was why most of them didn't make it past the first date, and Peter wondered if Ben was going to be just another in a long line of men who didn't want to understand. "No. I don't want to be a girl. I don't want to pretend to be a girl. I don't wear makeup or ladies' underwear." He grinned a little wickedly, leaned in a little closer, meeting Ben's eyes. "Or any underwear at all."

"So it's all about easy access?"

Peter was delighted. "That's one of the benefits."

"So why?" Ben insisted, and Peter was impressed. Not very many of them kept pushing—most decided it was easier not to know, easier to just wriggle out of dinner. Peter had started meeting them for drinks first to make it less awkward. Ben wasn't wriggling.

"Because I like the way it feels. I like the way it makes me feel."

"And how does it make you feel?" Oh, Ben was a smart one. More points for the older blond with the hint of crows' feet by his eyes.

"Sexy."

Ben grinned. "I can see that."

"Oh? You think it is, too?"

"No, I can see that it makes you feel that way. And I think that's exciting."

Peter smiled because he was hungry, for food and for touches that would lead to messy ends and the beginning of something real. Maybe he'd have it all with this man tonight...

"It's because the colour matches my eyes, isn't it?" he teases. Pushes. He can't help it, he wants to hear Ben say it. He doesn't need for Ben to be turned on by the dresses, but he wants Ben to be.

"Brat," Ben accuses fondly, hands sliding down Peter's legs and then back up them, beneath the dress. The thick fingers tease Peter's eager cock, Ben's thumbs sliding by his hips, dragging over his skin, and then Ben's hands come down again. "I got hard watching you put it on tonight. I've gotten hard watching you put on your dresses for the last few weeks."

"You never said anything."

"I didn't know if it would last. I wasn't sure..."

"That it was something you wanted to last?"

Ben nods. Always honest, his Ben, even when it isn't easy.

"And now?"

"Seeing you in a dress, in the right dress—I hated that red gauzy thing you wore the other night—arouses me. And it makes me hard, and it makes me want you."

Dinner had been a delight, the conversation varied and quick. Ben was an entertaining companion. And then they were back at Peter's place, mouths locked together, Ben pressing him up against his door. It felt good, being hard in this dress, feeling the hardness in Ben's pants pressing hotly against his belly.

"Let's get you out of this," murmured Ben, hands finding the zipper in the back and sliding it down.

The sound of it, the feeling of it made Peter shiver, his cock throbbing with anticipation.

"Does it turn you on?"

"You turn me on," Ben told him. "Because you're sexy and you know it. That look in your eyes, that makes me hard. Makes me want you naked so I can fuck you."

For tonight it was enough. Because Ben had asked the right questions and had stayed and wanted to make love to him, and that messy end was so close, the new beginning a little further away, but still within his reach.

"Do you want to fuck me in it?" Peter asks, both hands on Ben's face now, tilting it up so there's nowhere for Ben to look but in his eyes.

Ben shakes his head. "No, silly, I want to make love to you in it."

Oh. Oh, Ben has always been special, from that first night when he got hard, despite the dress, because of the way it made Peter feel. Now he is so far beyond special that Peter doesn't have the words for it.

Peter steps back, fingers slowly leaving Ben's face, and he backs up until the backs of his knees hit the bed. "So come make love to me."

Ben stands and comes to him, moving slowly, dropping his clothes as he goes. It isn't a striptease, but it does tease Peter, has him moaning and longing to touch the skin that's uncovered. He reaches out, and Ben steps into his arms, taking his mouth in a kiss that is slow and long and says everything that Peter has ever wanted to hear, all without words.

They move onto the bed, and Ben turns Peter gently onto his stomach and starts to kiss a trail down along his spine, leaving the silk damp and clinging slightly to his skin. It's arousing, this new thing that Ben does, it makes wearing the dress even better.

When Ben gets to Peter's ass, his tongue slides along Peter's crease and pushes against his hole. It makes him shiver and shake, makes him suddenly wish the dress wasn't there because Ben doing this is a magical thing and the silk is in the way now. Peter goes to pull the silk up over his ass, but Ben's fingers stop him.

"No, leave it be. I want to feel the silk around my cock while I'm inside you."

Peter gasps, his cock throbbing, the warmth in his stomach curling tight, making him shiver. He never would have thought of that, but now he wants it. "Please," he begs.

"Yeah. Yeah, just hold on." Ben opens the side table drawer and pulls out the tube of lube. It's battered and half used up; they make love a lot, fingers and bodies sticky and sweaty.

Ben kisses the side of Peter's mouth, and then he's behind Peter again, between his legs, face against his ass.

Ben's tongue pushes inside him, pushes the wet silk inside him. It drags against his skin, hot from Ben, delicate and rough at the same time in a strange but not bad way. Peter locks his elbows. He pants, rocking slightly, pushing back against the wet, hot invader.

Ben usually spends ages with that tongue inside Peter's body, revelling in it. Not today, though. All too soon Ben is pulling back, hand sliding up under Peter's dress, one slick finger teasing at his eager hole.

It doesn't take long at all, this familiar and intimate opening, stretching. And Ben has him rocking, has him moaning for it; those thick fingers know what they're doing.

Soon enough they're gone as well, and Peter whimpers, begs. "Please, Ben, please. I need you. Don't tease." He can feel the dress moving against his skin as he rocks, fucking the air with eager, hungry movements. "Ben."

"I'm right here. Gonna love you now. Love you just like you need."

Ben's hands are hot on his hips, holding him now as Ben's cock slides along his crack, so hot through the thin silk dress. So hot and yet so different from what Peter is used to. Then the head finds his entrance and Ben begins to push, the heat and silk breaching him.

Peter's groan is torn from him, the burn and stretch so familiar and, at the same time, so strange. The silk is nothing like a condom. It isn't like flesh either, or silicone, or anything he's ever felt inside him.

"Okay, Peter?" Ben's voice is tight, and Peter knows Ben needs to move. He also knows that Ben won't, not until Peter says he can. Peter squeezes, his body working around Ben's cock, making Ben moan.

"I'm good. It's good. Move. Please."

That's all Ben needs, and he's moving, pushing and pulling, hot and like silk—really silk—and it's different and strange and it's good and he doesn't want it to stop. He loves it, loves what it means, loves how the dress moves between them.

They rock together, moving together, and he doesn't want it to stop, this first time that Ben has found the dress sexy for itself.

But everything comes to an end and without Peter's cock even being touched he's coming, heat pouring from him, splashing against the front of his dress. His body squeezes Ben's cock, squeezes the silk-wrapped heat inside him.

Ben cries out, fingers hard on Peter's hips as heat fills him, spreading along the silk wrapped around Ben's cock. It is the most amazing sensation, and Peter just floats on it, on the satiation, the satisfaction that's moving from cell to cell, taking his whole body.

Ben pulls out, and Peter collapses.

Peter smiles as Ben carefully undresses him, pulling the silk off him with hands that know him, that love him, with or without his dress.

Ben lies down and tugs him into the curve of the long, strong body.

Peter smiles. "Love you."

"Love you, Peter."

They lie there for awhile, Ben humming now and then, just holding him. Peter thinks, drifting half asleep on the lassitude, the feelings like silk against his mind.

"Do you think it's because we've been together for so long?" Peter asks eventually, breaking the silence.

"What's that?"

"That you find it sexy now. That it turns you on. Do you think it would have happened even if you didn't know me—that you'd go out and look for someone who wore dresses?"

"Yeah. I never would have thought about it otherwise." Ben's voice rumbles beneath Peter's ear, low and warm and familiar.

"Oh."

"You're disappointed?"

Peter shrugs. "I don't know. I guess ... I don't know."

"Baby, I think you in a dress is exciting. It gets me hard. It makes me want you, makes me want to fuck you through the mattress, that dress hiked up over your thighs, your cock hard in my hand. What does it matter where it came from?"

Peter smiles and hugs Ben. "It doesn't," he says.

As he's drifting off to sleep he realizes that it's true.

Harold Hoefle

Running

The headmaster coughed.

"Boys, this is Rolland Krishan Salter, who comes to us all the way from BC. He brings great praise from his old school, so please welcome him to ours."

The headmaster applauded. Some boys traded looks; a few clapped. Rolland didn't move. Spiked black hair, light brown skin, six-two, and about 190 pounds, he stood still at the front of the airless room. Our school jacket pinched his bulk, and I could already see how his skin colour and style would exile him from our white-faced ranks.

Desks creaked as boys squirmed under his gaze. Finally, his blue eyes bearing straight ahead, he passed through two rows of stares to a desk near mine.

I was not built like Rolland. I was short and slight with red hair. He wouldn't know that the boys called me *leprechaun*, or that I ran cross-country. That I lived in a co-op with my divorced mother and attended the Academy on an Ontario Government bursary program set up for the *less fortunate*, a discreet program so boys like me could keep their dignity. My mother's finances and my own appearance, though, only partly explained why I couldn't look at another boy without thinking he was better.

The headmaster left, and our history teacher stepped up. Grinning, he asked if someone could define genocide. No-one raised a hand, so he started his list of slaughters. Outside, a wind moved the tops of birch trees encircling our school grounds. We slumped over our desks and closed our eyes, cradling our heads on our forearms.

"One million Armenians in 1915. Five to seven million Ukrainians in 1930-33. Six million Jews in World War Two. 800,000 Rwandans..." The squawk of the intercom woke us up. During the bulletin, we learned which practices began today. When the bell signalled the end of class, I stood by Rolland's desk.

"I'm Francis. Trying out for anything?"

He looked at me. "Do you remember your dreams?"

His voice was deep, a DJ's voice.

"Not often," I said.

Rolland nodded.

"Say you dream you're walking down a street and your head's on top of a mailbox, watching you. What would you do?"

"Talk to it? Hold it up?"

"I had that dream last night. My real face, and my eyes staring right at me."

"What'd you do?"

Rolland just stood up beside me. I saw crooked red lines in the whites of his eyes. Then someone laughed and shut the door. When I turned around, Rolland was staring at the wall.

Practice started by the football field, the trampled grass where boys smashed into skids of padded uprights. Stretching in the grass beyond the field, I was surprised to see him approach. Square shoulders, thick thighs, a gut edging over his waistband, Rolland looked even bigger in shorts and a T-shirt. Like a mountain. After he sat beside me he got into the hurdler's stretch, tucking his left leg behind him and extending his right. He struggled to grip his right ankle with his hands and bring his face down to his knee. He couldn't do it. He was stretching in the wrong grass for the wrong sport.

Coach Higgins, a gawky woman who taught Relations and Functions, tooted her whistle, and we gathered round. Noticing Rolland, she nodded. "Today, Francis will take the seniors for a ten-kilometre run. Juniors and bantams, stay with me."

I led our group to a ravine bike path. Soon Rolland's breathing grew choppy, so I slowed down the pace. Then the talk began.

"I met this chick on Friday night at Nick's. What a freak." Joey Spence, our best runner, picked up the pace. His arms swishing low at his sides, Joey did not actually run. He floated, like a hawk. But he was a pig.

"She was so out of it, bragging about places she'd screwed guys." Joey pressed a finger against one nostril and blew snot from the other. "The back of a bus, her school washroom, a pool..."

Everyone except Rolland and I snickered, and when he dropped back I went with him.

"Guys at your old school talk that way?"

"Most guys talk like that. So do chicks."

The others had stopped, and Joey stood apart, his hands clasped on his head as he moved his torso from side to side.

When we stopped, Joey looked at Rolland. "Something wrong?"

Rolland shrugged. "Girls don't interest me, at least not in that male-fantasy way."

"Are you saying you're a fag?"

"In Britain you'd be calling me a cigarette," Rolland said. "But *gay* is a better word. Less demeaning."

Distant traffic rumbled, and I didn't know where to look.

"You're joking," Joey said.

"Not about this." Rolland reached up and scratched the side of his head. He kept on doing it until Joey spoke again.

"You're admitting you suck cocks?" Joey said.

"And you lick clits. Or you'd like to. Who cares?"

Someone said, "Shit." A few guys kicked the grass, loosening some tufts. Everyone stared at the ground. Then we turned and started running, without Rolland. I glanced back and saw him standing on the path, his hands slack at his sides.

We ran fast, side by side, and everyone wanted to talk.

"I thought he was bluffing, but he's way too serious."

"Okay, so he's a fag, but who'd be stupid enough to say it?"

"He doesn't care—look how he insulted Joey."

"After Joey insulted him."

The talk worried me: because I was being quiet. Because I'd never had a girlfriend, and they all knew it.

"Some guy," I spat, "will beat the crap out of him."

Joey looked at me as his arms swung. He was hardly breathing.

"Francis, I know why you slowed down with him. I've seen you do other things."

"Francis isn't a fag. I saw him drool over that porno we had in class last year. Joey, that was the day you said you felt sick."

The guys laughed. We turned to go back, and I thought about meeting Rolland in the locker room. But when we arrived he wasn't there, and he didn't show up. I waited.

Before first period on the next day, one boy played prosecutor.

"Hey, Rolland, I heard you said you're gay. Are you?"

Rolland faced his accuser. "I thought cultured, private-school guys would consider sexual tendency a personal choice."

"He's dead," said a boy in the far row.

The teacher came in and scrawled his daily quotation on the board. *"To generalize is to be an idiot."—William Blake.*

Rolland raised his hand.

"Yes?"

"Sir, Blake is generalizing about people who generalize."

No-one even smirked.

In the following days, I watched Rolland as he sat in class or walked through the halls, meeting hate stares and averted faces, hearing names like *fag, queer, cocksucker.* And other messages were sent: boys graffitied his desk: *To tide you over, I brought you a cucumber. Spit or swallow?* Once, someone stuck a piece of paper that read *Make Gays Pay* onto the back of his jacket; another time, a boy horked from a landing as Rolland passed below, hitting his shoulder. He walked on.

Soon October came. The cold reddened our cheeks and the wind whipped the birch trees bare. The guys stopped tormenting Rolland. Perhaps the ability to abuse had bored even the abusers.

On a rainy Friday afternoon, the day before Halloween, the regional cross-country finals were held in a provincial park north of the city. Rolland finished an astonishing twenty-fifth out of ninety, sprinting past a runner in the last fifty metres of mud. I saw him cross the line and gasp for air, then he staggered into the chute and puked. I had placed eighth, Joey third. Our team came in second—its best showing ever. None of us had thought Rolland would crack the first sixty. Later, as we stood together in our sweats, Coach Higgins suggested a party at her house.

"Hey, Rolland," said Joey. "You have to go. I'll even swing by your place and, you know, pick you up." Everyone laughed. Except him. He looked past us at the grassy field and the other clumps of runners. When he saw us waiting for an answer, his face softened.

"Sorry. I've got plans."

"So cancel!" yelled Joey. "Let's party!"

Rolland closed his eyes. Then his face quickly changed, his eyes slitting as he glanced at us. The coach burst in on our talk and told us to get in the van. Later that night, driving home from the party in my mother's car, I stopped by Rolland's place.

***

A man with wet eyes opened the duplex door. He held a cigarette and a glass with a floating green rind.

I gave my name and asked for Rolland.

"Come in, Francis. I'm John, the father." He waved me inside. "The masochist went for another run. He's always trying to play the hero, ever since we came east."

A blur raced in through the door.

"Houdini! Behave when there's company." John giggled. "Rollie's new cat."

After taking my coat, John guided me to a lopsided wicker chair in the small living room. A fringed lamp sat on an end table, ceiling-high bookshelves stood against the far wall, and framed photographs covered the wall beside me. I saw a beach; a woman bent over green grass; a swarm of yellow butterflies. The photographs were framed in wood the colour of Rolland's skin.

"Ceylon," said John. "Also known as Sri Lanka. Heard of it?"

"It's near India?"

"Well done. Rolland was born there. His mother is from Tamil country. One morning, Rollie and I went outside and saw a man hanging from a lamppost. We left a week later." John swallowed the rest of his drink. "Francis, would you like a beer?"

I said yes, surprised by the offer.

Rolland came through the front door and into the room, sweat shining on his face. He wore a hooded YMCA-Vancouver sweatshirt. After nodding at me he took off his shoes and started stretching on the floor. He'd lost his gut. He looked lean, fit.

His dad brought me beer, and Rolland juice. John held a full glass of something clear against his chest.

"So, did you run hard?"

Rolland leaned forward to touch his toes. "You talk too much."

"At least I talk."

"Did you work today?"

John gulped his drink. "I ran errands and talked to a government fellow, about a contract in Nepal. Road construction. They need engineers."

"How many gins?"

"Come on, Rollie."

Rolland glared at his father until the older man walked away and closed the door behind him.

"You treat him like a kid," I said.

"He is a kid. He hasn't worked a day since Mother died in the war, over three years ago. He just watches TV."

I looked at more photographs while Rolland stretched. I saw pictures of a dark woman with purple and red flowers around her neck, a black ribbon twined in her hair. She was beautiful, but she never smiled.

When Rolland came over to me, his breathing made me tense. He kept looking at me in an odd, asking way. *Do something*, I shouted to myself. I was leaning closer, but he stayed still. It felt so strange: to know that at last I would touch someone who wouldn't flinch, who might let my hand linger on his arm, let me touch his face, a sweating face wanting what I wanted—

He pulled back.

"Dad always..."

Rolland mumbled something about his father and village women but stopped when he saw my stare. Then he went on, though I didn't hear a thing. I wanted to run away.

Rolland suddenly crouched down. He laced up his shoes, his hands shaking. Then he lifted his head.

"I didn't mean to upset you," I said. "I mean—you've got more courage than anyone I know."

"You," he said, and his voice stumbled. "You know nothing."

At the Halloween dance, I stood against the wall and listened to the DJ's awkward mix of droning heavy metal and pulsing dance tunes. In the dark gym I could barely see faces, just flashes of red, green, and yellow hair flying in the coloured lights. I hated dances. But I felt compelled to attend them, especially now. I had a reputation to uphold: The Normal Boy.

"Hey."

Joey's beery breath disgusted me. Still, I was pleased to see him. He rarely gave me more than a nod, in the halls or at practice. Though he had hugged me after the regional finals.

"Seen your special friend?" he said.

"Fuck you."

He grinned.

"Guess who's in a Tim Hortons downtown. With a girl in his lap."

The bass line of a song swam in my head. Bodies swayed near me, the pulse of bass guitar sending a human current across the floor. I wanted to join in, sink into the song, stretch out my arms and float until Rolland spilled out of my mind. But Joey grabbed my sleeve.

"He's not gay. It's all bullshit."

"Who'd pretend they're gay at a boys' school?"

He shook his head. "Jason's cousin went to Rolland's school in Vancouver. I was drinking at Jason's, and he told me what his cousin said. Rolland won his school the rugby cup. But at the victory party a guy touched him, and Rolland freaked, threw the guy head-first into a wall. Into a coma."

"That's insane."

"It gets insaner," Joey said, speaking into my ear. "After it happened, Rolland was in shock. Later he made a vow to his friends. If the kid survived the coma, Rolland would live somewhere else. And for a year he'd say he was gay."

I didn't believe any of it. I told Joey that.

"Francis, why would a huge rugby guy run cross-country? He *needs* to punish himself. Have you ever *seen* Rolland do something with a guy?" Joey's breath sprayed my face. "Has he tried to touch *you*?"

I knew that slapping Joey's cheek was the worst way to hit him— slaps were for girls. Faggots. But his words kept slamming into me, and I had to shut him up. When I hit him, he just laughed.

I walked to my mother's car, past some guys sharing a joint in the parking lot. Rolland had said I knew nothing. Maybe I did know nothing. But I could try to change that.

Rolland stopped coming to school, so I called. He said he'd been sick, felt okay now, but would take off one more day. When I suggested a run, he said he'd have his father's car the next night.

Rolland and I ran through the ravine, the lights of buildings and street lamps blinking from the distance, the dead leaves filling the air with a vegetal smell. We were running through a cool, dark, endless garden. A perfect place to talk. But I couldn't. *What*, I kept asking myself, *will I actually say?*

We neared the parking lot and the car.

I said: "Did you run for your school out west?"

"I played football and rugby."

"So why didn't you play football for us?"

Rolland said nothing and I looked over—he was staring straight ahead.

"Francis, I always had speed and desire. But if you want to be the best, you need cardio too. So you can rip down the field, again and again and again. I ran cross-country to get fit for rugby."

"Makes sense," I said, shaking out my arms. I felt alone.

After our run, Rolland opened the passenger door of his car. I started to get in, but he pulled me back and put his mouth on mine.

Rolland knew what to do next, in the dark, in the grass, away from everyone. I thought it would hurt and happen fast. I was wrong twice.

After a few hours of work in the UBC library, I return to my desk, turn on my computer, and there's an email from Joey, whom I haven't heard from in nearly five years.

But it's the subject header that catches my attention the most: *Rolland's accident.*

A cab hit him. The driver told police he was making a right turn in broad daylight when a young man ran in front of him. Joey learned about all this when he bumped into Rolland's father in a bar. The old man stank of booze, he said, and kept bragging about his son's *many talents.* Joey even went to see him at the hospital. He says *our friend's* condition has stabilized.

I watch the rain smear maple leaves over my office window, covering the glass with yellows and browns. Joey. Checking in with his guilt from the other end of the country. I almost fire an email back to tell him what Rolland did with me, and how he was being himself. But I don't write anything. Instead I recall that night, the grip of Rolland's hands as he held me, how I touched my own face and thought for the first time: *Now I matter.* And how, apart from the other sounds we sent into that night, he kept whispering a certain word. He spoke it so softly, I couldn't even tell if he was speaking English. Maybe it was Tamil, his mother's language. In any case, the word was one I didn't know.

JOEL HYNES

Lost Cause

Fourteen years old I was, first time I got a bit of skin. Whiskey had nothing to do with it either. Teresa Bennett. Me and Harold and another few b'ys were jiggin sea trout down off the breakwater when she come trudgin across the beach. Sixteen, I s'pose she was. Heavy too. She used to call me the lost cause.

—Here comes the little lost cause.

The big manly roars out of her then. It was a couple of years before I figured out she was just pokin fun at me name. And by that time she was dead. Killed. Loaded drunk and fell out the back of a truck near Bay Bulls somewhere. All of a sudden then everyone loved her.

That day on the beach she up and starts tossin rocks and chunks of driftwood out at our lines. Lookin to piss someone off. Askin for it. Harold called her an old slut and fired a rock at her. She slung one back, a big one, caught me right in the corner of the goddamn eye. An inch closer and I'da been the *real* hard ticket, right out of the movies, with the black eye-patch and the empty socket to show around at dances and shit. I never see it comin of course. I woulda got out of the goddamn way sure. But it knocked me down and the blood started streamin down me face. She laughed first. She did. Clear as day. But when she see the blood she got flustered a bit, started runnin towards me. I picked up a handful of rocks and let drift at her. She took off back up the beach and I took off after her. She was quick on her feet though, considering the size of her. But I s'pose she knew how cracked I was, split open and bleedin. I kept drillin rocks at her while I was runnin. She screamin back at me that she's sorry, that it was an accident, pleadin with me to fuck off. Blood runnin into me eyes, blindin me, the world coated muddy red. Cracked I was.

Teresa lumbers up the bank at the end of the beach, busts into the Reddy's old stage. No-one'd used it in years, 'cept for storin nets and gear. That's all anyone used 'em for since the plant opened up. Time I

117

gets to the door she has it barred off. She's all out of breath, I hears her tryna steady her lungs. I keeps heavin me shoulder into the door till I breaks one of the boards. I gives it one last go, exactly the same time she steps out of the way. I lands in on the floor then, and drives a fuck of a nail into me hand. That hurts worse than the rock in the face. She darts off to the other end of the stage but the back door's boarded up. I got her cornered. She knows she's in for it. Me there with me face all bust open and me hand gushin. She keeps on blubberin about how sorry she is and not to tell no-one.

—C'mon Jude, please...

And I realizes then and there that I've no clue what I'm plannin to do with her now that she's caught. I was just chasin her 'cause I was cracked. But now, when I sees her there like that with her big jugs heavin up and down and the sweat runnin off her forehead and her hair all plastered to it. And maybe the smell of the place too; fishy and damp and musty. And the dark of the room, little cracks of sunlight through the walls. I don't know, it's exciting. I picks up the handle of a gaff, holds it up to her face. She goes right quiet then. Just her breathin there. Dark patch of sweat on her chest. She makes a run, tries to get around me. I just shoves her down on top of the nets. I got a bit of height on her. One of her big jugs flops out of her bra. She looks back and forth from the gaff handle to me bloody head to the fresher blood drippin off me hand. She lies back, and don't think I'm not quick about it either. I got me lad out and in her before she can say me name. I'll give ya a lost cause, missus.

She never made no fuss, just lay there lookin at the wall. I got blood all over the side of her face and neck but she never made a peep. I got up then and I let her go on. I wasn't so cracked with her no more. Few days after I seen her walkin into her house and I went up and knocked on the door but she wouldn't come out. I s'pose where she was a bit older she didn't want no-one getting the wrong idea. Fuck her anyhow. Say nothing, saw wood.

'Bout a year after that I started knockin around with Margie Ryan. She was never with no-one before me, though. No. And of course I never let on about what Teresa Bennett went and done with me. Far as Margie was concerned, her first time was a first for me too. Still, I felt a bit cheated by the whole Teresa thing. And, to be honest, when she was tossed outta that truck down in Bay Bulls that time and cracked her neck and the whole Shore was getting on about what a lovely girl she was and how she never said boo to no-one, well I'd just have a glance in the mirror and I'd see this little scar in the corner of me eye and I remembers thinking to meself, well everything comes back to haunt you. She got hers, just like everyone else.

Yeah, I remembers thinkin that way alright...

Nalo Hopkinson

A Raggy Dog, a Shaggy Dog

There you are. Right on time. Yes, climb up here where we can see eye to eye. Look, see the nice plant, up on the night table? Come on. Yeah, that's better. I'm going to get off the bed and move around, but I'll do it really slowly, okay? Okay.

You know, I don't really mind when it's this hot. The orchids like it. Particularly when I make the ceiling sprinklers come on. It's pretty easy to do. I light a candle—one of the sootless types—climb up on a chair, and heat the sprinkler up good and hot. Like this. That way it only affects the sprinkler that actually feels the heat. Whoops, here comes the rain. Oh, you like it, too, huh? Isn't that nice?

Wow, that's loud. No, don't go! Come back, please. The noise won't hurt you. I won't hurt you.

Thank you.

I've gotten used to the sound of fire alarms honking. When the downpour starts, the orchids and I just sit in the apartment and enjoy it; the warmth, the artificial rain trickling down the backs of our necks. The orchids like it, so long as I let them dry out quickly afterwards; that way, it's a bit like their natural homes would be. When I move, I try to find buildings where the basement apartments aren't built to code; the law makes them put sprinklers in those units.

It's best to do the candle trick in the summer, like now. After the fire department has gone and the sprinkler has stopped, it's easy to dry off in summer's heat. In winter it takes longer, and it's cold. Some day I'll have my own rooms, empty save for orchids and my bed, and I'll be able to make it rain indoors as often as I like, and I won't have to move to a new apartment every time. My rooms will be in a big house, where I'll live with someone who doesn't think I'm weird for sleeping with the orchids.

My name is Tammy. Griggs. You can probably see that I'm fat. But maybe that doesn't mean anything to you. Me, I think it's pretty cool.

Lots of surface for my tattoos. This one, here on my thigh? It's a Dendrobium findlayanum. I like its pale purple colour. I have a real one, in that hanging pot up there. It looks pretty good right now. In the cooler months, it starts dropping its leaves. Not really a great orchid to have in people's offices, because when the leaves fall off, they think it's because you aren't taking care of it, and sometimes they refuse to pay you. That's what I do to earn a living: I'm the one who makes those expensive living plant arrangements you see in office buildings. I go in every week and care for them. I have a bunch of clients all over the city. I've created mini jungles all over this city, with tropical orchids in them.

This tat here on my belly is the Catasetum integerrimum. Some people think it's ugly. Looks like clumps of little green men in shrouds. Tiny green deaths, coming for you. They're cool, though. So dignified. To me they look like monks, some kind of green order of them, going to sing matins. After their singing, maybe they work in the gardens, tending the flowers and the tomatoes.

On my left bicep is the Blue Drago. They call it blue, but really it's pale purple, too, like the Dendrobium. This tat underneath it is a picture of my last boyfriend, Sam. He drew it, and he put it on me. He did all these tattoos on me, in fact. Sam was really talented. He smelled good, like guy jizz and cigarettes. And he would read to me. Newspaper articles, goofy stuff on the backs of cereal boxes, anything. His voice was raspy. Made me feel all melty inside. He draws all the time. He's going to be a comics artist. His own stuff, indie stuff, not the superhero crap. I wanted him to tattoo me all over. But he'd only done a few when he started saying that the tattoos freaked him out. He said that at night he could smell them on my skin, smell the orchids of ink flowering. Got to where he wouldn't go anywhere near the real plants. He wanted me to stop working with them, to get a different kind of job. You ever had to choose between two things you love? Sam's dating some guy named Walid now. I hang out with them sometimes. Walid says if he ever gets a tat, it'll be a simple one, like a heart or something, with Sam's name on it, right on his butt. A dead tattoo. When Walid talks about it, Sam just gazes at him, struck dumb with love. I really miss Sam.

I think the orchids, the real ones, like me fat, too, like Sam did. Sometimes at night, when I've turned off the light and I'm naked in bed—those are rubber sheets, they're waterproof—and I can see only the faint glow of the paler orchids, I swear that they all incline their blooms toward me, toward my round shoulders, breasts and belly, which also glow a little in the dark. We make echoes, they and I. I *like* to smell them; the sweet ones, even the weird ones. Did you know that there's an orchid that smells like carrion? I stick my nose right in it and inhale. It smells so bad, it's good. Like a dog sniffing another dog's butt. Yeah, you'll get to do your trick soon. You've been trained well, haven't you?

Hear that? It's the fire trucks coming. Time to get ready. You going to follow me? Yes, like that. Cool. I'm just going to grab the bigger plants first, put all my babies into the bathtub where they'll be safe. I have to move quickly. The firemen will burst in here soon, and they aren't too careful about pots of flowers. I learned that the hard way; lost a beautiful Paph once, a spicerianum. The great lump of a fireman stepped right into the pot. He asked me out, that guy did, after he and his buddies had made sure nothing was on fire. His name was Aleksandr, Sasha for short. I don't get how you get "Sasha" from "Aleksandr," but that's what he said. He and I dated a couple of times. I even went home with him once. Sasha was nice. He liked it when I sucked on his bottom lip. But I couldn't get used to the dry feel of his cotton sheets, and I had to stop seeing him anyway; he'd have begun to get suspicious that the fire trucks kept being called to wherever I lived. I need a handsome butch bottom or a sweet misfit guy who doesn't care how often I move house. Someone strong, but with a delicate touch, for staking the smaller orchids and, well, for other stuff. I think the next person I pick up will be like a street punk or something who doesn't even have a home, so she or he won't barely notice that I have a new flop every few months.

Yeah, it's really wet in here now, isn't it? I'm just going to grab that Lycaste behind you, then put all the plants under the grow lights so they'll dry out. Don't want them to get crown rot. Okay, let's go. Oh, I nearly forgot my new baby! Yeah, it's a pain to carry. The vine's probably about seven feet long now. You can't tell cause I have it all curled up. Its flowers aren't quite open yet. I need to take it with us, and a few other little things.

This way. Follow the plant.

I have a routine. Once the plants are safe, I go out into the hallway. No-one ever notices. Most of the tenants are usually down in the street already, standing in their nightclothes, clutching their cats and their computers. I'm soaking wet, but, if anyone asks, I'll just tell them that the sprinklers came on, that I don't know why. People expect a chick to be dumb about things like that. I'm careful, though. Almost no electricals in my apartment. Electricity and water don't play nicely together. I use candles a lot. The grow lights for the orchids are in the bathroom, and I don't activate the sprinkler in there.

This apartment building has a secret. It's this door here, between the garbage chute and the elevator. The lock's loose. Going through this door takes me right up the secret stairs to the roof. The firemen probably won't even look there. If they did, I'd just say that I got scared and confused, just picked a door that had no smoke behind it. Yeah, you have to come up. It's where the plant's going, see?

I'm going to miss this place, with its quiet asphalt roof. This is the second time since I've been here that I've sprinklered the plants, so it's time to move on. I don't like being such a nuisance to the neighbours. One time, in another building, I flooded the apartment beside mine. Ruined the guy's record collection. Made me feel really bad.

Up here it stays warm all night, and slightly sticky. I think it's the heat of the day's sun that does it, makes the asphalt just a little bit tacky. Sometimes I lie out here naked, staring up at the stars. When I roll over, there are little rocks stuck to my back, glued there by warmed asphalt. I flex my shoulders and shake my whole body to make them fall off. I like the tickling sensation they make as they come loose.

It's pretty up here tonight. You can see so many stars.

The other night, I put two blue orchid petals right on my pillow, with a petal from one of them under my tongue for good measure. It tasted like baby powder, or babies. That's a joke. Because I've got this spiky green hair and the ring through my lip, some people can't tell when I'm joking. They think that people who make holes in their bodies must be angry all the time.

I'd found the orchid petals just lying on the ground out back of my building, by the dumpster. Didn't know who would tear orchids up that way. Lots of people keep them in their apartments, or grow them competitively. The climate here is all wrong for tropical orchids, yet I bet there are almost as many growing in this city as you'd find in any jungle.

Anyway, that night, I laid my left ear—the left side of the body is magic, you know—on the fleshy, cool blue of the orchid petals, closed my eyes, and waited for sleep. I sucked on the petal in my mouth. They were a weird, intense kind of blue, like you get in those flower shops where they dye their orchids. They cut the stems and put the flowers in blue ink, or food colouring. The plant sucks it up, and pretty soon the petals go blue. You can even see veins of blue in the leaves. This orchid had that fake kind of colour.

Not sure why I did that with the petals. You know how it is when you see a dog that someone has tied up outside in the cold, and it's shivering and lifting its paws to keep them from freezing, and all you really want is to saw that chain off and hug that cold dog and give it something warm to eat? Well, actually, you may not know what that's like. You'd probably rather bite a dog than cuddle it. But I'd seen those torn orchid bits lying there, and I just wanted to hold them close to me. So there I was, with two inky orchid petals crushed between my ear and my pillow, and one under my tongue. It looked like a vanilla orchid, except for being blue.

I think I nodded off. I must have, because after awhile I saw a rat crawling in the open window.

I didn't want to move. From snout to tail tip, it was the length of my forearm. I could see its pointy teeth glinting—the front ones, the ones that grow and grow, so that rats must always have something on which to gnaw, or those teeth grow through their lips and seal their mouths shut, and they starve to death. Its teeth gleamed yellow-white, like some of my orchids, like my belly where the skin isn't inked.

So I didn't move. Anyway, I was dreaming. No, stay away from the flower. I know it's almost daylight, but it's not quite ready yet. It blooms in early morning, and I think this is the morning it will open completely. I guess you can tell, and that's why you came.

Anyway, in my dream, I watched while the rat climbed around my orchid pots, investigating. Some of the plants it peered at, then ignored. It only seemed interested in the ones with flowers on them. Those it sniffed at. Maybe rats don't have too good eyesight, huh? Maybe they go more by a sense of smell? Not sure how it could tell how anything smelled, cause its own smell was pretty foul. Like rotting garbage, climbing around my room. Could smell it in my sleep.

Finally, the rat seemed to find what it wanted. It nosed at my Vanilla planifolia. I was proud of that vine; it was big and healthy, and some of its flowers had just opened a few hours before. The rat climbed up onto the vine, made its way to one of the flowers, and stuck its head inside the bloom. Then it climbed back down again and made its way to my window. It stood in the window for a second, shuffling back and forth as though it was unhappy. Then it leapt out the open window and was gone. And this is how I knew for certain that I was dreaming; when the rat jumped, I saw that it had wings. Gossamer wings, kind of like a dragonfly's, with traceries of veins running through. Only more flexible.

That woke me right up. I sat up in bed, feeling really weird, and all I could think was, with four legs and two wings, doesn't that make six limbs? And wouldn't that be an insect, not a rat?

There was another thing, too. I couldn't be sure, because it had happened so quickly, but I thought the rat's wings had had a faint blueishness to them.

I got myself a glass of water and went back to bed. Next morning, the flower of my lovely Vanilla, the one the rat had rubbed itself on, was beginning to brown. That was odd, but not too strange; vanilla flowers close within a few hours and fall off if they're not pollinated. But now it also had a faint scent of dumpster garbage in the summer heat. Never smelt anything like it on a planifolia. Some people would say that's gross. To me, it smelt like a living thing, calling out. Scent is a message. Sam used to like to sniff my armpits when we fucked. I wonder if he sniffs Walid's?

Look, you can see the firemen milling around outside now. That's the super; the woman with the bright yellow bathrobe. Even in the dark at this distance, you can see that it's yellow. Matter of fact, everything she wears is yellow—everything. I've seen her doing her laundry, and, yep, even her undies are yellow. Weird, huh? Yellow is a screaming kind of colour. Not like blue, which is so restful. Though maybe you don't like blue very much right now.

She's just let the firemen in. They'll go and break into my apartment, but they won't find anything.

I think the bud's beginning to open. No, you can't rub yourself on it yet. Oh, poor little guy; you're really only about half rat anymore, aren't you? You've got orchid tendrils growing up into your brain cells. Does it frighten you, I wonder? Do you have the part of your brain left that can get frightened? I don't think you wanted to jump off that ledge that night, but I think the orchid made you do it. Phew, you stink! I know it's pheromones though, not real garbage.

Even though I told myself I'd been dreaming, I closed my window from that night on. Then a little while ago I stopped to hang with

Micheline. She hooks on my street corner on weekend nights; teaching grad school doesn't earn her enough to make ends meet. Sometimes, when business is slow for her, she'll buy me a coffee at the corner coffee shop, or I'll buy her one, depending on which one of us got paid most recently. She told me the oddest thing; how the street kids are starting to tell stories that they've been seeing angels in the city. It's getting to be the end of days, the kids say, and the angels are here to take all the street kids away to Heaven. The angels are small and fuzzy, and they have sharp teeth and see-through wings.

You know, I don't know how I'll ever find someone like Sam again. You'd think I'd have plenty of chances. I go out into the world every day, I meet people, I'm friendly, I'm cute—if you like your girls big and round and freaky, and there's those that do. I get dates all the time. Smart people, interesting people. But it's so hard to find people I click with. They just, I dunno, they don't smell right, or something.

The great thing about orchids is that they have a million ways of getting pollinated. They trick all kinds of small creatures into collecting their pollen and passing it off to other orchids: wasps, ants, even bats. Bee orchids produce flowers that look like sexy lady bees, and when a male bee lands on the flower, ready for action, he gets covered in pollen. A Porroglossum will actually snap shut for a few seconds on an insect that stumbles among its blossoms; it'll hold the insect still, just long enough for pollen to rub off on its body. Some of the Bulbophyllum smell like carrion so they can attract flies.

Us, all us orchid nuts who bring tropical orchids into places where they don't grow naturally, and who cultivate them and interbreed them, we're creating hothouse breeds that thrive in apartments, in greenhouses, in office buildings, in flower shops—all behind doors. They need to find each other to breed. They need pollinators. And what small animals get everywhere in a city?

Yes, you, my ugly, furry friend. You only want me for my orchid. Actually, you want me for *your* orchid, the one that's learned how to travel to where the other orchids are. Most bizarre adaptation I've ever seen. It must have gotten seeds into your fur. Some of those seeds must have germinated, put roots down into your bloodstream. I thought it was wings I saw when you jumped from my window, but it was really the outer petals of the flower, flaring out from your chest in the wind from your jump. It's a stunning blue, for all that it stinks. True blue orchids are rare. Lots of people have tried making blue hybrids. I went and looked it up. One thing they might try soon is to make a transgenic plant by incorporating enzymes found in the livers of animals. The enzymes can create a bright blue colour. They react with something in the plant called *indoles*. They regulate the growth of orchids. D'you know one of the places you can find indoles? We put them in the packing mixture we use to transport orchid plants in, to keep them healthy. Your plant passenger there has tendrils in your liver, my friend. When you eat, it gets fed. I can see that you've got a new bloom on your chest there. I wish I could saw your chain off, but it goes too deep inside you. I can't save you the way I'd save a dog.

Maybe the plant didn't get the knack of it the first time. Maybe when the first bright blue blossom opened, you tore it out, petal by petal, before it could mature into its garbage smell. But eventually one of the plants put roots down into your spine, travelled up to your brain, found the right synapses to tickle, and you lost the urge to destroy it. Lost the will to go about your own business. Now you can only fetch and carry for a plant, go about the business of orchid pollination. Do you know that *orchid* means *testicle*?

My flower's opened all the way. Cool. Yes, I know you can tell; look how agitated you're getting, or at least the orchid part of your brain is. Don't worry. I'll let you at it soon.

There's a story that some people from India tell. If you want to bond a person to you forever, you have to prepare rice for them. While it's boiling, you have to squat with your naked genitals over the pot. The steam from the cooking rice will heat you up, and you'll sweat salty crotch sweat pheromones into the pot to flavour it. Make someone eat a meal with that sweat rice, and they're yours forever. Orchids and dogs would understand that trick. Scent is a message.

Here. Come on over. Come to the flower. No, I'm not going to step away from it. You have to come to us. Gotcha! Don't bite me, you little devil! There. A snootful of chloroform ought to do it.

Jeez, I hope you don't die. I think I got the dosage right; you can find anything on the web. I just don't want this to hurt you, or you to hurt me because you're scared. Look, I even brought cotton batting to keep you warm in while I do it. Good thing Sam taught me how to do a little bit of tattooing. Just inside your ear should work. Not much fur there, so it's likely that somebody will see it.

Oo, that ear's disgusting. Glad I brought some alcohol swabs with me. Thank Heaven for the gloves, too.

There we go. There's not even a lot of blood. Your ear membranes are too thin to have many blood vessels.

You poor thing. First a chunk of your brain gets kidnapped by a flower with a massive reproductive urge, and now a human being is having her way with you. And you smell like wet garbage in the sun. But for you, that part's probably a plus. Probably gets you all kinds of rat dates. I just want a chance, too. Want to send out my own love notes, on as many channels as I can. I mean, who knows where you go in your travels? You might end up in some kind of horticultural lab, and a cute scientist might find you and see your tattoo.

Huh. You're a she-rat. Sorry, sister.

I place personal ads, I dress nicely, I chat people up. Nothing. Plants, they just send their messages out on the wind, or via pollen stuck to an insect, or if they're this puppy, they travel a-ratback to wherever their mates are likely to be. Human beings only have a few options. And even pheromones only work so-so with us. Never can tell if the message will get through. So I'm doing everything I can to increase my chances.

There you go, sweetie—the date, my name, my email address, and the name of the new subspecies of orchid that's flowering there on your tummy; V. planifolia var. griggsanum, after me, who discovered it first.

Please don't go into shock. I think you should be warm enough wrapped up in the cotton. I'll keep dribbling some water on your tongue, keep you hydrated until you wake up. Lemme just have a quick look at this bloom on your chest ... God, that's creepy.

The firemen are gone now. Pretty soon I'll go in and start packing. I've already put down first and last month's rent on a little place in the market; one of those trendy new lofts they've been putting there recently. It's got the right kind of sprinkler system in all the units. It's probably already got vermin, too, being in the market, but that's okay. The more of you I can find and tattoo, the better. Rats don't live very long, and I bet orchid-infested rats live even shorter than that.

Oh, hey. You're awake. Good girl. No, no, it's okay. I won't hurt you. The pot's here, with the flower in it, and I'll just step away from it, okay? All the way over here, see? And I won't even move. Yes, you go ahead. Go and pollinate that baby. Though if it can be pollinated, it's no baby.

I didn't squat over a boiling pot of food; I made my room steamy hot, and squatted over an orchid plant—that one right there that you're currently rubbing your body against. Watched my sweat drip into the moss in which it's planted. My calf muscles were burning from the effort by the time I straightened up. That plant's been growing in a medium impregnated with my pheromones. It's exchanging scent messages with your flower right now. Anything that might work, right? You're done? You're leaving? That's okay. Just climb down carefully this time. We're way high up. Atta girl, carry my message; fetch!

No Parking

She was driving one of those discreetly expensive cars—a person could mistake it for a Volvo if they didn't know better, but I knew cars. She got out of her Renault and gave my co-worker Steve a hug. I wondered how a babe like her knew a loser like him. He was a pasty-faced guy whose jeans and T-shirts were always on the crusty side, as if every morning he spilled cereal on them. He'd finished high school eight years earlier and been working at the garage ever since—for a buck over minimum wage. He thought he was going to make it in the music biz. Please.

She was a classic beauty: Catherine Deneuve in *The Hunger*. Her face was fleshier and heavier at the jaw than Deneuve's, but I liked that. She seemed sensuous; I could imagine her slurping down oysters and kissing me greedily. She was pretty-in-punk: tall and curvy, long blond hair with black streaks, wearing a black mini-dress with ripped black tights and scuffed army boots. I also wore army boots but never dresses. When she disappeared into the lower depths of the parking garage, I scooted out of my booth and over to Steve.

"Who's that chick you were talking to? She looks really familiar," I lied. Steve knew I was gay, but I didn't want him to tell his friend, who was probably straight, that a dyke he worked with had the hots for her.

"Nathalie? She used to hang out with my brother. She wants to take pictures of my band for some kind of project." Steve winked at me. "Sexy, eh?"

I hadn't fooled him. "Think she'd want to take pictures for my zine?" I put out an independent magazine called *Girls with Guitars*. "Could you introduce us when she leaves?"

"No problem, dude." Being called *dude* gave me a thrill and notched up my respect for him.

Steve stretched his neck farther out of his booth to speak to me in a lower tone. "She likes chicks."

"She does?" My heart jammed like I had taken speed.

Nathalie drove through my booth an hour later while Steve was arguing with a customer, so I introduced myself to her and babbled about my zine. She listened attentively, making no attempt to rush off. I gave her my phone number when I noticed a bumper-car scenario beginning to happen as cars in my line tried to pull over to Steve's booth. She handed me a ticket for a show she was going to the next night.

"Thanks." I shoved the ticket into my pocket. "If I'm not working, I'll check it out."

I acted really cool, but I could not believe my luck. It was like getting a date with the prom queen, except she had more of an edge: more high-school slut than cheerleader. She had to know I was a dyke. Since I had shaved my head and started dressing in black Levis and plaid shirts with the sleeves cut, straight people assumed I was a man, fags hit on me like I was a twink until their eyes hit my crotch, but queer women recognized me as one of their own.

The next night I turned up at the club, a place with dark walls, no windows, and a black shag carpet on the floor strewn with ashes and cigarette butts. It was like walking on a giant expanse of pubic hair infested with crabs. The band playing on the riser at the back was a metal/funk group with four white guys. The bass player was getting a good freak on, and I watched his hands as they slapped and tickled his instrument. He both worshipped and possessed his instrument. I wished I could jam like him, make my hands fly without thinking about what I was doing.

I arrived late—I hated waiting for girls. As I had hoped, Nathalie was already there. She looked super-cool. She had on the same torn tights and army boots as the day before, but instead of a mini-dress she wore a tank top and tiny black cut offs with *FUCK* sloppily sewn on the back left pocket and *OFF* on the back right. I smiled when I read the message. I drank a couple bottles of beer and checked out her sexy ass, which was pouty yet firm. She ran around and talked to various guys, a big camera swinging from her neck. She took some pictures of the band, and finally, she came over to me. She kissed me hello on both cheeks.

She slid into the back booth I had scoped out, sat very close to me, and put her camera on the table. She stared at the band while I peeled the label off my beer bottle. When the set ended, she asked me what kind of pictures I needed for my zine.

The truth was I did not need a photographer. I had one, Liz, an artist who also did collages of mutants, little girls, and Siamese twins that cracked the edge of cute. But I had to tell Nathalie something, so I suggested she take pictures of all-girl bands.

"All-girl bands?" Nathalie sneered. "Like who? There's Dairy Queen—but Cat, their lead singer, fucking hates my guts. You know what she said to me once? She said, 'Nathalie, you take pictures of boys because you don't know how to be in the picture.' All because I once slept with a guy she was in love with."

Cat's voice sounded like a distraught chipmunk's, but Dairy Queen were great eye candy. Too bad Nathalie wasn't on better terms with them.

Nathalie leaned over so her face was closer to mine. Her grey eyes were flecked with light—polished spoons. She sniffed. "You know, you smell like tea."

Tea? That was so crunchy. I wanted to smell like sin. "It's sandal-wood."

"Maybe I'm getting confused between some tea and some incense I bought at the health-food store."

I felt relieved, then awkward. I had managed to remove my beer label intact, and I folded it into a square. I hated the beginning part of getting to know someone. But I rarely got past that way-too-familiar experience. I'd had a few flings since I'd come out, but only one steady lover, and she had split her time between me and a guy, then dumped both of us for a woman whom even I mistook for a man.

"Hi, Nathalie." A tall, thin boy wearing a long black leather coat stood in front of us holding a pitcher of beer in one hand and two glasses in the other. Goth Boy stared intently at Nathalie with his eyeliner-rimmed eyes.

"Salut, James." Nathalie avoided his gaze, but she bumped her hip against mine to move over and make room for him. After I slid over, she fastened her hip more closely to mine and opened her palm in my direction. "This is Nicky, the woman with the zine I was telling you about."

"What's it called?" James put a bony hand on her arm but she shrugged it away. We were all skinny and hardly took up half of the large, dark vinyl booth, and yet I felt like I had no room. We were three burning matches in a box.

"*Girls with Guitars,*" I said.

"Never heard of it." James tucked his long hair behind an ear. "And

I'm in a band, so I read music zines."

"It's a queer riot-girl zine, so I'm not surprised." I wanted to get the lesbian thing out in the open and make him realize he wasn't the only one who had a potential claim on Nathalie. If Nathalie had been with a guy, James never would have sat down without asking.

"Riot girl, eh? I support the movement. Too bad most of the bands suck," James said.

"Yeah, like most punk bands are so great," I retorted.

"What bands are you talking about? I don't think I've actually heard a riot-girl band." Nathalie said while she poured a beer for him in one of the glasses he had brought over and a second one which she set between us.

"I guess you're not into feminism." James gave us both a fat smirk.

"I've been away for two years," Nathalie snapped.

"Oh yeah. With André." James looked away from her and drank his beer.

The band started again, and I was happy to have an excuse not to talk to him. Maybe Nathalie was, too. I put my hand on her thigh and began tracing the seams of her shorts with my fingers. I wanted her ass across my lap and her shorts pulled down. The slogan on the back pockets of her shorts was far from original, but it was effective. She was the haughty girl that guys liked to claim "provoked" them—an attitude to which I had expected to be superior, but I realized instead I felt like just as much of a thug. I curled my fingers into a fist, jamming them between Nathalie's legs while she bit her lip. When she slunk down to allow me to touch more of her, I rolled my knuckles back and forth and snuck a look at James. I didn't think he knew what was going on but I didn't care if he did. Getting to do what I wanted turned me on.

When he got up to get more beer, Nathalie purred, "It's sexy when you sneak around."

I pulled my hand away. "Is James your boyfriend?"

"No. My lover. *Was* my lover. I dumped him last night."

I hadn't expected that. Emotions I might have felt toward her puckered like skin in the cold. Did she expect us to fight over her? I said nothing, but my face must have because when she started talking again, her tone was defensive.

"He saw me in the lineup of a club and decided I was the girl for him. He's an idiot. He doesn't know me, but he thinks he's in love with me. I told him I had a boyfriend, but that didn't matter to him. So we had a fling."

She had a boyfriend. Her parking lot was full. Did I leave or drive around? In my experience, it's always best to drive around. A space could open up, be yours if you grabbed it before the other guy circling around did.

"André and I are breaking up, but we still live together. I don't have the money right now to get my own place."

At the end of the evening, I shared a cab with Nathalie. She complained a lot about André, but she went home to him.

A few days later Nathalie drove her Renault into my parking garage. I didn't notice her until she knocked on the glass door of my booth. I let her in. Seeing Nathalie in the daytime felt strange. The booze and dark club had made conversation easy and intimate. Now she acted as if we were old pals. She sat on the only seat, a stool, and talked to me about travelling in Asia, where she and André had taught English in Korea and Japan, then used their savings to hang out in Thailand and Bali. She missed travelling; it took her out of herself and made the club scene seem irrelevant. She read a lot of books while travelling, stuff on Zen Buddhism, the history of Cambodia and Japan, art. Reading kept her from having to deal with her boyfriend.

"Why'd you go to Asia with him?" I asked.

"To get away from my boyfriend before him." Nathalie fidgeted with some woven Guatemalan bracelets on her slender arm. "I was in a relationship with this guy who wouldn't let go. He was stalking me, and I had to get a restraining order against him."

Men, men, men. "Have you ever had a relationship with a woman?" I asked.

"I dated this girl when I was nineteen, but she was a troublemaker. She was really macho. It was okay for awhile, but I used to be afraid she would get too drunk one night, call my family, and tell them I was a lesbian."

For some reason, I remembered the first time I kissed a girl, back in ninth grade at a sleepover party. Truth, dare, double-dare, promise-to-repeat. *Dare. I dare you to kiss me.* I'd poked my tongue through lips that tasted like Double Bubble gum and drew away from mine. *Ew, why'd you french me?* I'd protested that it was a game, but fear lobbed around my brain.

"Do you get a lunch break?" Nathalie was looking me straight in the eye.

Steve covered for me for half an hour while I followed Nathalie down a level to her car. She got into the driver's seat, reached over, and opened the passenger door for me to get in.

"There's some pot in the glove compartment," she said.

I clicked open the lid, and car registration papers fell onto my lap. I picked them up and put them back in the glove compartment, noticing as I did that André was the owner of the Renault. I found a small baggie of pot and handed it to Nathalie. She rolled us a joint and lit it using the dashboard lighter. As she handed me the spliff, she said, "You know, it was refreshing to have someone not be shocked when I told them I was stalked. Or, worse, feel sorry for me."

I nodded before inhaling. I, too, hated having people feel sorry for me, although it didn't happen often.

I pinched the joint after we had smoked about half of it. The weed was good quality, and I didn't want to get too wasted since I had to work. Nathalie, sprawled next to me in a stupid torpor, didn't protest. My eyes fuzzily followed her collarbone down to an edge of black lace cupping her breasts. Her beauty was intimidating, but I was a woman who took dares, so I put my arms around her and kissed her. She didn't put her tongue in my mouth, but she kept her mouth open and wound her hands around my neck. After awhile, she pushed me against the seat. She was very quiet, which made me nervous. Was she enjoying herself?

She pulled my T-shirt up over my braless breasts, exposing them.

"God, I could kill you—you have the breasts of a teenage girl." Nathalie leaned back into the driver's seat, surveying me.

You're supposed to want my breasts, not want to have them, I thought. I felt the unseen presence of a man in her mind—for whom we were performing and competing.

"Whenever I have sex with André, I feel like he should have breasts," Nathalie said.

An unwelcome image of Nathalie running her hands through the chest hair of a naked guy rolled through my mind. I distracted myself by reaching behind her and unzipping her black cotton dress. I leisurely brushed each of her shoulder straps down and unhooked her bra. She had the kind of body some women get surgery for. Her nipples were large and pale as sand dollars, and I leaned over and took one of them into my mouth, sucking it into a pink tip. Then I kissed the other breast. Nathalie's breath sharpened, and she moved her head from side to side. But then she drew away and zipped her dress back up. She leaned over, cupped my face in her hands, and kissed me so softly that I knew it was over—whatever it was.

I went on a lot of dates with Nathalie over the next couple months, but we didn't have sex. We went drinking at straight bars where Nathalie knew a lot of boys-in-bands who talked to her about *making it, really making it, not just in Québec or Canada, but in LA, man.* I tolerated this, barely. I had to worry more about strange boys flirting with her than about the man with whom she lived. She was such a shit to him: we'd be talking on the phone, and she'd put down the receiver to yell at him for not buying the right brand of soy milk for her. I wasn't concerned about her running off with another woman: she had no female friends, and she was always putting down the various girls in the music scene. I kept waiting for her to put me down, too.

As the months passed, I stopped being afraid she would run away. The problem was she stayed in place. When were we going to do more than make out? Did she not want me the way she wanted men? Her ambivalence kept my own desire in check.

One night we ran into my co-worker Steve and the rest of his band, the Dead Brain Cells. I had seen them play before but had never met the rest of them personally. Nathalie knew them and introduced me to everyone as "my friend Nicky." As she chatted with the guys, I stewed over the fact that she had pointedly called me her *friend.* We were more than. Tonight I was going to pin her down on what exactly we were— after I had a few drinks.

The Dead Brain Cells didn't talk to Nathalie for long; they were on their way to a gig. As they walked away from us, both Nathalie and I overheard one of them say to Steve: "How do you know that fag she's with?"

Another guy chimed in, in falsetto: "Is there something you're not telling us?"

"Nicky's a girl I work with, not a guy." Steve increased his pace.

"Tabarnac!" Nathalie gave me an apologetic look.

I shrugged. They were dickheads, but I was used to that sort of thing: homophobic ripples in my day. I didn't usually get hassled when

I was with Nathalie. Her beauty buffered me from the snarky comments of straight guys and the glares of straight chicks when I went to the bathroom in a het bar. I decided to take advantage of Nathalie feeling bad: "I want to go to a dyke bar tonight."

"Well, okay."

"What's the matter?"

"The music will suck." Nathalie wrinkled her nose.

She was right, but I wanted to be around my tribe. I also wanted to run into my ex-girlfriend. I hadn't spoken to my ex in months, even though she wanted us to be friends. I thought I might be able to manage to speak to her with Nathalie pinned to me like a corsage. Nathalie was better-looking than my ex.

Nathalie and I walked over to Huis Clos, a lesbian cocktail bar named after the Jean-Paul Sartre play. The bar had originally been a first-floor apartment built in the early part of the twentieth century. The outside of the building was smooth, grey stone flanked by large stained-glass windows. Inside, the bar was small—the regulation pool table barely fit into the back. You had to ask someone to move every time you took a shot. There was no dance floor, but the bartender had a boom box that played Dionne Warwick and Grace Jones.

"I like this place. I've never been here before." Nathalie arranged herself on a high bar stool.

I stood beside her, leaning across the bar to pay for our drinks. After I tipped the bartender, I scanned the room for my ex but instead caught Liz's eye. She was wearing a gingham dress, and her dark, crimped hair was pulled into two braided pigtails fastened by bright red baubles. She never dressed like a normal person; she showed up to everything in a costume. She cared more about art than about looking sexy. She came over to where I was standing and rested her scarred elbows on the edge of the bar.

"You know, Liz, you kind of look like Dorothy from *The Wizard of Oz*."

"Oh goodie," she said without irony.

"Guess you're not in Kansas anymore." I tossed my head in the direction of all the women surrounding us. Neither Nathalie nor Liz smiled. "The Tin Man was my favourite character. What about you guys?"

"The Wicked Witch," Nathalie said. She sipped her Campari and lime through a straw. "I mean, Dorothy was pretty boring, always whining to go home. How pathetic is that? I'd like nothing better than to get the fuck out of here and travel to Asia again."

I leaned back and rested my elbows against the bar. Her words stung; I was part of here.

Liz put her head in her hands, then looked up. "Toto. I liked Toto."

"By the way, I'm Nathalie." Nathalie proffered her hand to Liz, who clasped it heartily.

"Sorry, I forgot my manners." I edged my tongue around my teeth—it felt as if something was caught but I could find nothing. "Nathalie, this is Liz. She does art for my zine."

"Are you Nicky's girlfriend?" Liz ducked her head slightly.

"Kind of." Nathalie kept her tone light.

"I guess I'll see you guys around." Liz slid her elbows from the bar. I would not say she disappeared into the crowd—not in that outfit—but she moved away from us.

Nathalie poked my bicep with the straw from her drink. "You know, I usually can't tell when an Anglophone wants to go to bed with someone, but that girl has a kick on you."

I shrugged. I knew Liz liked me, but I ignored it. Liz was so awkward. She couldn't make the patter a woman needed to survive and make friends in the dyke bars. She was a talented artist but too weird for me. I told Nathalie, "I'm not sure if she wants to have sex with me, but I think she might want to lie down naked together in a field and put body paint on me."

Nathalie snickered.

I took a sip of my beer. "What did you mean about not knowing when an English person wants to sleep with you?"

Nathalie laughed and an unexpected dimple appeared high on her cheek. "If you go to bed with a Francophone, he will tell you, 'I like your toes. You have beautiful breasts. I love you. I love you.' He will be tender, whereas English guys often don't talk—it's a cliché, but they are more reserved, in my experience. I can always tell when a French guy is flirting with me, but I'm never sure with an English guy."

I polished off the rest of my beer and set the bottle down with a clink. Was she trying to tell me something? I didn't tell her she was beautiful, but I often reassured her. Told her that her clothes looked great, that she was not having a bad hair day, that she didn't look fat. Didn't she understand how I felt about her?

"When are you going to sleep with me?" I wanted to sound seductive, but a whine crept into my tone.

"Can't we just let it happen if it happens?"

"That's not good enough." Anger edged into my voice. "Either you want to or you don't." I glanced away from her, toward the women standing at the bar, and tried to find a cutie I could imagine doing, but it didn't work. I couldn't escape the humiliating situation I had put myself in as I waited for her to say something.

"Alright. Let's go to your place now. I can't spend the night, though." Nathalie refused to look at me, just gulped down the rest of her drink. We left the bar and hailed a cab from the street. She got into the front of the cab, leaving me to get into the back by myself even though I was the one who directed the cab driver. I felt like I was bringing a prostitute home. Not that I ever had, but that's what popped into my head.

When we got to my apartment, Nathalie surveyed my living room and made the joke everyone did about how it looked like I had just moved in. Most of my furniture and utensils were stuff you used when you went camping. I had visited her place last week when André was at work. Their apartment had a definite look—something that had clearly required a lot of effort. The rooms were painted yellow and burgundy and olive with many carved mahogany boxes and chests that I later found out were Balinese. There were glass jars filled with marbles, leafy plants on antique oak plant stands, and pillows covered in Thai silk. If Nathalie was planning to move out of that apartment, she was not leaving soon.

I went into the kitchen to fix us some drinks and was surprised, when I came out, to find her lying in my bed, under the covers but clearly naked. I would have preferred to have undressed her myself, but I didn't say anything. I set our drinks on the floor, got under the covers with her and nibbled her neck, which was acrid with smoke. She slipped her hands under my T-shirt and began to pull it over my head. I let her take my shirt off, exposing my breasts, but when she started undoing my belt buckle, I stopped her. She was moving too fast, and I wasn't ready. I wasn't sure I could be ready. I was scared to let her do something to me and then notice that she found it gross. She never talked about women, about wanting them. It was always men, men, men.

"I want to fuck you," I told her, while hoping that saying it would make me want to. I had never been so nervous with a woman. I put my thumb under her chin and tilted her head back. I remembered her saying she liked bad boys in bed, nasty motherfuckers, as she disconcertingly called them, so I tried to be that bad boy. I sucked her nipples, pulled her hair, and then spread her open and sucked her clit. The noises she made were slight, barely encouraging, so I stopped. She had left a streak of wetness on my chin, however, so I began to fuck her with my hand. When she groaned, I felt relieved. I tucked all of my fingers and thumb into her and wished I had an expensive latex dildo. I wondered if she would like it or find it stupid and fake compared to a guy? After a few minutes, she pushed her cunt over my knuckles and squirmed in a quick orgasm. My own response was more cerebral: pride at making her come rather than being turned on myself.

She lay still, and then rolled over and asked if there was anything she could do for me. I shook my head because I could not get over this feeling that she would just be doing me as a favour. I had thought that making her come would make everything right—affirm that, yes, she wanted to be doing this, that she wanted to be with me—but her coming cracked apart whatever there was between us.

"I should go. André..." Nathalie let the sentence trail off as she shoved her dress and panties back on and laced up her army boots. She put her bra in the pocket of her leather jacket.

"I'll walk you to the metro."

As we walked to the subway, Nathalie chattered about how impossible it was go to shopping with her mother, who bought her clothes that were ugly and too large and who complained about her daughter's weight. "She wants me to be fat like her," Nathalie said with disgust.

I felt annoyed, distant. What did she care if someone else was fat? The gap between us reminded me of seventh grade when all the girls in my class stopped playing games, training-bra mania began, and I just didn't get it.

When we got to the stairs leading down to the metro, I leaned over to kiss her but she pulled away.

"Don't. Someone ... one of André's friends could see us."

After that, I didn't call her and she didn't call me. Two weeks had passed when Steve came up to me while I was on break, reading next to the Coke machine.

"So you're not seeing Nathalie anymore," he said.

"Yeah, well, she's straight. That's the last time I go out with a straight chick." I continued to look at my book as if I were reading, but I couldn't concentrate. Was Nathalie a lesbian? I just knew how equivocal her desire for me had felt. Nathalie competed with other women and was scared shitless to be a dyke, but that didn't mean she wasn't one.

Steve's Coke clanged to the bottom of the machine but he ignored it. "That's not what I heard. She said you acted aggressive, like a guy"— here he waggled his eyebrows so I'd know that he knew she meant *in bed*—"and that was the last thing she wanted or expected from a woman."

"Bullshit!" I stood up, and my book fell to the ground. I was aghast that she had told him such intimate details. My hand squeezed into a fist, and I pounded the Coke machine.

"Hey. Don't shoot the messenger." Steve bent over and pulled out his Coke. His jeans were too big around his skinny waist, and I could see half his butt.

"If I was a guy, we wouldn't be having this conversation." I picked up my book and stamped back to my booth. Thinking about her and her boyfriend that she pretended wasn't her boyfriend pissed me off. André was seven years older than she was and had a decent job. Nathalie liked his money, liked having a car. No way would I let her park that Renault in my garage again. If she tried, I would fold my arms across my chest and say, "Pardonnez-moi, mademoiselle, stationnement interdit pour vous."

I expected to run into Nathalie sooner or later, probably in a bar on St. Laurent, but less than a week after my conversation with Steve I saw her downtown. I was on my bike, coming home from work. The streets were crammed and noisy. It was Grand Prix weekend, Montreal's Formula One racing event. There was a certain irony to having a car race in the middle of a smog alert, but nobody seemed to care. I stopped at a red light, then noticed Nathalie getting out of the passenger seat of the car beside me. The Renault was parked illegally. When the driver got out, Nathalie pointed to the sign at the corner. He squinted at it, gave her a naughty-boy grin, and then shrugged his shoulders.

"André!" Her frustration pierced the sluggish air. She drew glances from passersby, and not just for her looks.

Her boyfriend was blond and handsome, a fraternity brother in rumpled khaki shorts. I had expected him to be dull, proper, a suit with a humiliatingly large bald spot. Instead, he and Nathalie were attractive enough to appear on reality TV. Neither of them appeared to notice me.

"Nathalie," I called.

Her eyes met mine. She didn't move, but she looked like she wanted to steal off.

I dragged my bike over to the curb where she and André were standing. She had humiliated me at work; now it was her turn to suffer.

"What are you doing downtown?" I spoke to her with a rough intimacy, as if she was a teenager, and I was her father who had a right to know her business.

"André wants to see the new collection of Ferraris." She shifted her body so she was facing away from me.

André stuck out his hand. "Hi there. Don't think we've met. I'm André." His grip was professionally firm.

"Nice to meet you." I gave Nathalie an expectant stare.

"This is Nicky, a friend." Her tone was infused with a blandness that suggested she barely knew me. Francophones were expert at using politeness to convey disdain.

My heart hopscotched. "Yeah, right. Friends call each other when they have something to say. And friends don't fuck."

Nathalie gasped, but it was André's reaction that I watched: his silky smile fading; the pinch of his eyes as he appraised me before concluding my threat level was green: low risk, but measures were required. He grabbed Nathalie's arm. "Payback for Namiko?"

She slammed her elbow backwards, ripping her arm from his grasp. "Not everything's about you, you know." She scowled at both of us. "You two should sleep together."

André flung his hand back, scowling at her. He didn't say it, but the word *bitch* was all over his face.

Nathalie walked away, twisting purposefully through the crowd and putting as much distance as possible from where she had been standing with me and André. He got back into his car and blasted his horn to pry a space through the people scrambling around, the long honks signalling his anger. I stood on the sidewalk, ignoring the hostile stares of pedestrians annoyed that my bike was blocking their progress.

Jingle Balls

I've always had a Santa Claus fetish. The sight and sound of a red-clothed, pot-bellied man shouting "Ho-ho-ho" sets my skin on fire. Panting, I ogle the suit's plush, velvety fabric edged tantalizingly with strips of white animal fur, which hide nothing but cling voluptuously to every curve on Santa's massive, flesh-packed body. His sheer girth gives him a presence other men lack. The deep, thundering, ultra-masculine voice issues from far inside his vat-thick chest. When he laughs, every inch of his body trembles spectacularly.

Right out front, the overconspicuous, rectangular, silver belt-buckle just begs to be undone; below, his gigantic stomping boots hint at the magnitude of other members. Above, a gleaming pom-pom dangles from a cap tip that bends like a half-erect penis. His blindingly white hair cascades in swirling waves down his head and shoulders, around his face. His glinting ice-blue eyes, looking into mine, seem to pierce my very centre.

My knees give out. With eyes closed, I imagine I'm pressing my mouth against his white glove, softer than anything I've ever touched.

My fuck-buddies barely put up with me.

"I have to wear this red hat with the little ball on it?"

"Quit calling me Kris Kringle; my name's Steve."

"But I don't want to say 'Ho-ho-ho' when I come."

"Okay, if I promise to give you a truck set, will you get off my lap?"

I'm not the only one who loves Santa, and I wish other men had the guts to admit it. Once at a Queer Nation meeting the talk turned to alternative sexual practices, and I finally said, "Alright, I want every guy here who's honest and horny to stand up and say, 'I want to be Santa's butt-boy.'"

People looked at their feet, and one guy started talking about golden showers. Imbeciles!

I'm the only person who wears a Santa suit in the Gay Pride parade.

I even carry a sign, "Santa's little helpers want blow jobs."

Once I went to *The Barn* in my Santa suit on fetish night. Approaching the bouncer at the door, I adjusted my belt and made sure my beard was straight. "Ho-ho-ho, little boy. Have you been naughty or nice?" He glared back. "Only leather allowed."

Why is our community so bloody conformist? Do all our desires have to be identical? It'd be like discovering every package on Santa's sleigh contained the same thing, or like opening a present and seeing you got the same dildo you were given last year and that again your parents forgot to include the two AA batteries, so you can't play with it right away or demonstrate it to all your aunts and uncles who will be arriving for turkey dinner in about an hour.

Because Christmas, everyone knows, is the most erotic time of the year. Listen to the carol lyrics: "Come all ye faithful," "Shepherds quake at the sight"; orgasm-imitating "Pa-rupa-pum-pum"s and "fa-la-la-la-la"s fill the air. Ripping off November's calendar page to reveal December is like tearing off a man's jockstrap. Streets are lined with long, twinkling, phallic strings of lights, dangling mistletoe forces total strangers to lock lips, while seductive Santas rhythmically ring large, clangorous bells on streetcorners, or sit glaring from plush department store thrones, emitting such blistering sexual energy, only children are allowed to approach and touch them. All around, swirling, burgeoning throngs of frenzied, panting shoppers heave bags bulging with wrapped packages that will be shaken and fondled by the hands of their trembling, curiosity-wracked recipients. The pandemonium and tumult increase until December 24th, when Santa finally blows his load, and we wake up to stockings crammed full of liquorice whips, half-naked tin soldiers, dick-long candy-canes, and mountains of presents in irresistibly lurid, shiny paper that our nails tear, gash, lacerate, and shred. Pine trees become penises pointing at the sky; Christmas wreaths hang like giant cock rings. Once at Aunt Mildred's, as I reached for the cranberry sauce, it all became too much: I raced into the empty study where I pulled out my engorged penis and ejaculated all over the walnut-wood Nativity Scene. "Joy to the World, the Lord is Come." Christmas is the most wonderful time of the year.

But afterwards, when the room is littered with torn wrapping paper, dismembered GI Joe limbs, and crumpled paper cups from *Pot of Gold* chocolates, and your mother says she found the bill for the S&M dungeon set that came with pieces missing, you immediately realize: Santa didn't bring any of these things—your parents bought everything.

I understood all this the Christmas I turned thirty, as I stood staring at myself in the mirror, my Santa beard coming unglued. I thought: construction worker fetishists have real construction workers they can lust after. Guys into uniforms can chase cops who are actually cops.

Did Santa really exist?

From the depths of my being, a voice suddenly rose, boomed loud, definite, and incontrovertible, saying, "YES, Virginia, there IS a Santa Claus. He will bring you all the joy of Christmas—and rip your underwear off with his teeth."

It was then I understood why Santa never visited me: he thought I didn't believe in him, and up until then perhaps I truly hadn't—or, like everybody else, I ignored his needs and was fast asleep when he arrived, leaving him not so much as an *Inches* magazine he could jack off to.

The next week I went to the library to do some research. When I saw the first known picture of Kris Kringle, I swooned. "Born in 1793, young Kris showed a propensity toward generosity and comforting the sick and needy." He stands in youthful splendour, gleefully carrying firewood into a family's home. The wife's dark eyes smoulder as he passes. Looking closely you can see that her husband, watching young Kris, has a bulge in his pants. Kris could satisfy in every way possible. The last authentic picture was from 1840, "when he was granted eternal life in exchange for all his kindness." After that, there were no more Santa sightings. Perhaps people were tired of him, or thought he was too old to be any fun, so he stopped visiting and remained at the North Pole. Why cross the whole world if all you're gonna get is a glass of warm milk and a few goddamned cookies?

Yet, in the final portrait you can see a tortured, clenched look in his eyes; Santa has needs that aren't being satisfied, desires that Mrs. Claus, the elves, and his reindeer know nothing about.

Santa, if I could take you in my arms, the heat from our bodies would melt all the snow in the vast Arctic land where you live, and together we could discover the true meaning of Christmas.

The time had come for direct action. January 1, 1996, was the day I began writing raunchy letters to the North Pole. I enclosed nude photos of myself. I sent one each month, then one a week, then one every day.

At the summer solstice, I faced north in an empty field and sang as loudly as I could, "I Saw Mommy Rimming Santa Claus."

The months passed, Christmas came and went, but there was no Santa anywhere.

I redoubled my efforts. I lay awake at nights calling out his name. I'd gaze out my bedroom window, which faces north, and say clearly, "You see me when I'm sleeping, Santa. You know when I'm awake. You see me now, you wild untamed thing. Come, I want you."

I had my chimney widened for easier access and the roof flattened, so there'd be no danger of the sleigh toppling into my neighbour's rose bushes.

"Santa, tonight's a sex party," I intoned. "I'm the only adult left who believes in you, the only person who wants more than toys. Only I will hold your magic penis in my hands, rubbing it like kindling to create a fire that will consume us both. And remember, Nicky, I'm only mortal and can't wait forever. Strike while the testes are hot."

I sometimes wondered if between my intellect and desire there was a tiny gap where disbelief lodged. I investigated my inner self and found that, no, I couldn't believe more. I knew that when we want something badly enough, the world molds itself to our desires.

Then, finally, Christmas Eve 1997. At exactly midnight I heard, coming from above, bells jingling and the crack of a whip. The sound vanished.

I ran to the window, but it was too late.

The next morning I discovered that the top of the alder tree had been knocked off, and my neighbour was screaming because there was shit all over his patio. The police came to investigate, and, yes, it was reindeer excrement.

I went out back and stood gazing at a steaming turd as one would at a religious relic.

I was stunned, could not speak for almost a week.

For the following twelve months I thought about Santa every day.

The next Christmas: again, bells jingling; but this time I thought I caught sight of a sleigh vanishing in the sky.

What was I doing wrong? Why wouldn't Santa come in?

At last on December 24, 1999, 11:55 PM, as I stared at the milk and cookies, I had a revelation. I leaped up, flung the tray aside and replaced it with a bottle of lube and foot-high piles of condoms.

Suddenly, a clattering on the roof.

The creak of the chimney lid opening. A boot kicking, then sheet metal rattling. The clatter descended, grew louder, and suddenly Santa was there, right in my living room. He stood in front of the fireplace, smiling.

I nearly fainted. I took a deep breath and, leaning against the sofa back, steadied myself.

I gazed into his ice-blue eyes and finally said, "Santa, I've been a good little boy."

"I know you have," he replied warmly. "Thanks for the invite. It's nice to know some people still want it."

He touched his belt buckle and instantly, as if by magic, was completely naked. His pale stomach rose like a magnificent iceberg, and his erect penis was as red as Rudolph's nose.

"I'm your Christmas present," I said. "Unwrap me."

"Thank God," he cried, approaching. "I haven't had sex in 150 years."

He threw me under the Christmas tree, and, as he tore my clothes off, a choir started singing "Gloria in Excelsis Deo." Above my head our gyrating bodies were reflected in a trembling silver ornament.

My mouth wandered over Santa, enjoying all his startling flavours— it was like biting into *Pot of Gold* chocolates after misplacing the flavour chart, being repeatedly surprised at the unexpected tastes: the delightful butter-mocha, the thrilling cashew cluster.

Soon Santa started thrusting, crying out, "On Donner, on Comet, on Cupid, on Blitzen." When he came, it was like a shower of presents falling from the sky. He did it again and again. I kept switching positions: up, down, over, under. My body became the world, sometimes Asia, then Africa, North America, Antarctica, and all night Santa travelled over it, depositing his gifts everywhere; 150 years of locked-in Santa sperm were released into the biosphere. Never had I dreamed of such a white Christmas.

The grandfather clock struck four, and I saw the room was piled to the ceiling with presents, the hanging stockings so full the seams had burst.

Santa abruptly got up and said, "I must go." In one second he was completely dressed.

"Go?" I said breathless. "Go? But are you coming back next year?"

"If you want me to."

"And the year after and the year after?" The words exploded from me. "Santa you must, you must!" Listening, he gathered up his empty sacks and his whip. "And I promise, I promise to be a good little boy all year. I'll only have sex using condoms and try to come at the same time as the person I'm with and never leave before he's come and I'll masturbate every day to keep my forearm muscles strong and never surreptitiously spit out another man's cum but either swallow it or splatter it out dramatically across his chest."

Santa smiled and, with his rosy red cheeks, looked for a second just like the picture on my grandma's cookie tin.

"Wonderful. I'll be so happy to see you." He stepped into the chimney.

"And don't feel guilty about visiting only once a year. I'm somewhat commitment-phobic, and a long-distance relationship suits me just fine."

I ran forward and bit into the seat of his trousers, so that when he ascended the chimney I went up along with him. On the roof the reindeer lay panting: they'd been humping, too. Steam wafted from their bodies, half the snow was melted, and Rudolph's red nose was completely brown.

Santa sat in the sleigh. He quickly tapped the whip handle on the chimney and the deer assembled.

"Ho-ho-ho," he bellowed as the sleigh rose into the air.

I stood waving. I cried, "Bye, Santa. I love you!"

Just for a second I saw, outlined against the full moon, the rows of reindeer, legs moving in perfect unison, the sleigh with curlicues above its runners, and the small, still form of Santa seated, one arm raised.

And I heard him exclaim as he rode out of sight, "Merry Christmas to all, and to all a good night!"

Ray Vukcevich

Strong Suits

One day Jack Spangler got bonked on the head by a person or persons unknown, robbed, and left for dead. Meanwhile, back at the apartment, Danielle tossed her things into suitcases and split. She was long gone by the time Jack got home from the hospital minus his memory. She'd deliberately left her business suits behind, abandoning everything they represented, but the suits had become so accustomed to life in the fast lane that they refused to just give up and hang there.

They would impersonate her.

They found and destroyed the note she left for Jack. The note had said, "Jack, I'm sorry, but I've gone off to find myself. Maybe I'll paint or blow glass. See if you can find someone who can use my girl lawyer suits. I'll probably never be back. Love, Danielle."

Home again after three days in the hospital, Jack was all khakis and blue shirt and a white X marking the spot on the back of his head where the blow had been struck. His kind of memory loss meant he could remember almost everything about the world and how it worked, but he had no clue about his place in it. He didn't even feel comfortable with his name. Jack Spangler. How could he be sure that was his name? Was he really a well-known cook? Who had that been on the phone telling him he should take all the time he needed and not worry about coming back to the restaurant? Maybe it was all code. Maybe he was a government witness or a retired spy or a professional killer.

His doctor told him watch for anything out of the ordinary. How would he know what was ordinary and what was not? Good question, his doctor said.

Were the suits out of the ordinary? Or should he think of her as the Suit since they were, in fact, all aspects of the one woman who had probably once eaten a lot more than she did now, coming home from the law office and dropping her briefcase on the floor and as often as not making straight for the closet, where she would hang muttering or softly snoring until it was time to get up and go litigate some more the next day? The Suits always had things to say to him when addressed directly, but they were baffling things that he didn't know how to respond to, since he was not sure what his relationship actually was to this multifaceted creature.

Once after the Suit of the day had flapped off to work, Jack crept into the closet and sat on the floor and felt the rest of the skirts brushing his face as they shifted around, gossiping and complaining about how they had no support systems, no jeans, no T-shirts, no underwear, no tennis shoes, no little black dress, no Bermuda shorts, no hats, no scarves, no pastel bracelets with progressive slogans etched into them, no bottles, no tubes, nothing on the top of the dresser. Nothing whatever pink.

Jack listened carefully, hoping for clues.

There were no clues.

He prowled around the apartment trying to remember what he should be doing. The other Suits joked or bickered, laughed and cried, and sometimes they enticed him into the bedroom to tease him, but mostly they ignored him.

Then the working Suit came home and joined the others.

He listened to them in there until he couldn't take it any longer. Then he rushed to the closet and jerked open the door, and they went silent, and their silence meant *So, what do you want now, Jack?*

He didn't know.

Next to the Grey Suit, who had had a hard day, there was the Navy Suit, who loved the late afternoon and early evening meetings and cocktails after work, and the Tan Suit, who lived right on the razor's edge of making a joke—no, no, she never would, but you always thought she might—and the Black Suit, who probably took too much pleasure in the kill. Jack loved their straight skirts and double-breasted, tailored jackets—no pants, never pants, and when it came to hats and gloves, well, you've got to be kidding, right?

"Let me in," he said and put his hands on the hangers of the Suits in the middle and pushed them aside.

"Hey! Hey!"

"Watch it!"

"So, this is cozy, right?"

"Cozy."

"We have a man in the middle."

"All hot and hairy."

"Did he shower today?"

"My guess is no."

"No, you're quite wrong! He did indeed shower."

"Not that it did him any good."

Jack gave it up and moved away and closed the door on their giggling.

"Oh, Jack. Jack," they called after him. "Don't be like that."

He made a salad of fresh spinach, radishes, cherry tomatoes, and goat cheese. He cut a few slices of bread from the loaf he had baked earlier in the morning. He decanted the wine and set the table.

He grilled a couple of lamb chops.

Would the smell tempt her? No, of course it wouldn't. He cooked, but she never ate. It was a subtle rejection of the very core of his being as a cook.

He sat down in front of his food and picked up his fork.

"Jack?"

She was grey in the bedroom doorway. She had no expression for him to read. He could make nothing of her contours. Late evening sunlight through the bedroom window outlined her and sparkled like jewels around the top of her collar. The shadows were missing beneath her skirt, where her legs did not go all the way down to the floor. For the first time, he might have thought that strange, but she said his name again, and he threw down his napkin and got up and came across the room to her. He put his hands on her waist and pulled her in close. He was confused all the time, but he knew he loved her several selves, colour-coded and accessorized. She drove him crazy, but he knew he was in the right place as she leaned into him with no weight, some swishing, maybe a small sigh like an oyster burping politely. She smelled like wool and plastic buttons.

"Hungry?" he said, nuzzling around her collar. When she stiffened in his arms, he said, "Oh, never mind. We could watch TV. Or play Scrabble. Come talk to me."

He wanted to talk about his day and the way things came back to him and then flew away again. He wanted to hear about her day. He wanted there to be some part of the day that belonged to both of them. He had so many questions. He might ask if she had any exciting cases ongoing. Or do we have children? What's up with The Goofball in DC?

What's your favourite colour? What are we going to do about world hunger? Where did we meet? Is there rain in the forecast? Do you love me even a little bit?

She worked her way out of his arms.

"Don't ask," she said, and turned away from him and fluttered back to the closet, where she joined the others.

He couldn't go back to his dinner. He couldn't watch TV and pretend they weren't in there talking about him. He decided to go out for cigarettes.

But once out on the sidewalk he realized he didn't smoke and didn't want to start smoking now. Hey, he could go down to the restaurant. Why not? Maybe the place would trigger something in his memory. He should go back up to the apartment and get his knives. He had knives? Yes, he had knives. But he wouldn't need them tonight. Unless he was not really a chef at all and this fascination with slicing and dicing indicated something other than food preparation.

No. He stopped suddenly on the sidewalk and people grumbled at him as they moved around him. No. His blade work was a source of pride.

And the blade work all had to do with food.

This business of being a serial killer or a CIA operative was nonsense. He was a cook.

He remembered telling Danielle exactly that. Had it been their second date? She was going to be a famous lawyer. I'll always be a cook, he said. Maybe I'll work my way up to a classier joint, but if you get tangled up with me, you'd better like to eat.

Oh, I like to eat, she told him with a sly smile.

He could see that smile now, just the smile, the cat was still missing, and hadn't her legs gone all the way down to the ground back in college?

It was not that she had changed, he realized with a chill of despair. She was simply gone.

He turned to go back the way he'd come and realized that he'd gone too far. Nothing looked familiar. He had no idea how to get back to Danielle.

Faces swooped in at him from the fog that was also setting summer sunlight. He radiated panic, and the open space around him widened as the people trying to get home after a long day moved away from him. He pulled himself into himself, folded himself once, twice, turned down his edges so no-one could see what was happening inside. They wouldn't like it if they could see that. They might have him arrested, hauled off the street, locked up, and then he'd never get back to her. He should play it cool. He should stop making those blubbery sounds.

Yes, stop. And when he was still, everything stopped.

Time itself stopped.

And then it started up again, and Jack saw Louie's Meat Market and knew exactly where he was. In fact, he was amazed that he had ever been confused. He was about five blocks from home. The sun had gone down, so he could not judge how long he had been out in the street. Probably not days. He walked back to his building and up to the apartment.

The bedroom door was closed. He put his ear against it, but he heard nothing. He opened the door expecting sulking darkness, but the lights were all on. The closet door was open a little, but not enough for him to see what was going on in there. There were the rustling, whispering sounds of conversation—probably a conspiracy.

There was a trail of clothes, like breadcrumbs to the closet. Jeans. Underwear. A pink T-shirt, yellow sandals, and something white that might have been a crumpled tissue but seemed more substantial. He picked it up.

It was a sock. There was a cartoon moose on one side and a squirrel or beaver on the other. The squirrel was wearing a leather helmet with goggles. He knew he should know these animals. He knew they were important to everything that had happened to him in the last few weeks and might be the key to everything that was about to happen to him now as he reached for the half-closed closet door, which, just before he touched it, swung open, and the Black Suit stepped out.

"Jack!" she said.

"You're going out?"

"I'm home," she said. "When you weren't here, I called Roland at the firm and made arrangements to meet him for drinks to mend my fences, but I can do that tomorrow!"

She came into his arms, and he moved with her to the bed, doing a dance step from the last century. Oh, maybe there were still ballroom occasions when such a step might be appropriate—and situations like this. It was the perfect move at a time like this.

He lowered her onto the bed and put his hand beneath her skirt and felt her great emptiness, so smooth and perfect. He pushed her skirt up and up and felt her absence pulling at him. He broke away breathing in little gasps and cries and jumped out of his khakis and blue shirt, black socks, and underwear. Her skirt was bunched about her waist. Her jacket and blouse were open. He swooped down on her, and they spun away together, and he entered her void and was suspended in nothingness for a moment, and then she moved against him, and then they moved together, stuff and no stuff, yin and yang, light and dark. Hello, goodbye.

This is much better, said the whole universe, and he said, yes, I agree completely. He was everywhere. He was everything. He had no questions.

Well, maybe one.

Like what's this?

Flesh around the edges.

A woman developing like a photograph in a chemical bubble bath. Champagne and sweet smile and sleepy eyes.

And ears.

Who knew she had ears?

Well, she must have had ears beneath all that reddish hair back in the days of ragged jeans and an abbreviated shirt with some kind of design on the front, maybe somebody's interpretation of a sunset or the startling consequences of projectile vomiting a pepperoni pizza. No, no, not that, she smells too good, no wool, no plastic. As she comes around the fountain, he can see she's holding a guitar by the neck like something she's chased down and killed for lunch.

Looking at him.

Looking at me?

I'm Danielle, and I'm going to be a famous lawyer some day soon.

I'm Jack, and that same day of which you speak I'll still be slinging hash. Well, maybe a better grade of hash. Would you like to come up and see my chef's hat?

And then he was not everywhere but just here, entirely here. He shuddered to a stop, and the suits in the closet sighed—a sound of sadness and completion.

"That was wonderful," the woman said, "if maybe a little desperate. I guess you missed me?"

There was a light scattering a freckles down her right shoulder, and, if we were past the jacket but only still working on the blouse buttons in that complicated procedure of getting her out of her business suit, you might wonder how far those freckles went—not so far as the lovely breast, and oh, look, there was a similar but lighter scattering of freckles on her left shoulder, too.

Clavicle. Surely that was the kind of word that would get you naughty websites if you googled it.

He kissed her throat.

"They said you'd been hurt," she said. "They said something about your memory. I turned around and came back as soon as I heard."

In the same way he had seen her develop from the emptiness of her suit into what she now was beneath him, warm and squirmy, with both hands on his chest pushing him up so she could get a good look at him, he saw a realization grow in her eyes.

"You don't remember me!" She sounded a little frightened. She would be thinking she had just made love to a stranger. She would be thinking that had probably been the reason he had seemed so totally frisky himself—she was a stranger, too. It was the old "strangers on a train" routine. Had he ever mentioned that fantasy? Hey, wait a minute, that wasn't even his fantasy.

It was hers.

Danielle.

He put his hands on her shoulders and glided them down her body like a blind man, over her hips and down her legs. He put his hands under her knees and pushed them back up toward her chest. Houston, we have feet. Amazing. The right foot. The left foot. But what's this? He grabbed her left ankle with both hands.

"Jack?"

She was still wearing one white sock.

Moose and squirrel.

"Bullwinkle!" he said, and everything came back to him. "Where have you been, Danielle?"

"Dude ranch," she said.

And later, after they'd showered and she'd called Roland to apologize, he cleaned up the remains of the dinner he hadn't eaten anyway and made a light pasta dish and a fruit dessert. He opened a different wine. He told her he could tell she hadn't been eating right, but he didn't tell her the way he knew was the fast-food undertone to her breath.

She told him about the dude ranch, the horses, the campfires, the tequila, the singing. She was sorry she'd been out in the woods when word came of his injury.

He told her what he remembered about the mugging and about his days with the Suits.

He left out a lot of details.

HOLLY PHILLIPS

Virgin of the Sands

Graham came out of the desert leaving most of his men dead behind him. He debriefed, he bathed, he dressed in a borrowed uniform, and without food, without rest, though he needed both, he went to see the girl.

The army had found her rooms in a shambling mud-brick compound shaded by palms. She was young, God knew, too young, but powerful: her rooms had a private entrance, and there was no guard to watch who came and went. Graham left the motor-pool driver at the east side of the market and walked through the labyrinth of goats, cotton, chickens, dates, and oranges to her door. The afternoon was amber with heat, the air a stinking resin caught with flies. Nothing like the dry furnace blast of the wadi where his squad had been ambushed and killed. He knocked, stupid with thirst, and wondered if she was home.

She was.

Tentative, always, their first touch: her fingertips on his bare arm, her mouth as heavy with grief as with desire. She knew, then. He bent his face to hers and felt the dampness of a recent bath. She smelled of well water and ancient spice. They hung a moment, barely touching, only their breath mingling and her fingers brushing his skin, and then he took her mouth, and drank.

"I'm sorry," she said, after.

He lay across her bed, bound to exhaustion, awaiting release. "We walked right into them," he said, eyes closed. "Walked right into their guns."

"I'm sorry."

She sounded so unhappy. He reached for her with a blind hand. "Not your fault. The dead can't tell you everything."

She laid her palm across his, her touch still cool despite the sweat that soaked her sheets. "I know."

"They expect too much of you." By *they* he meant the generals.

When she said nothing he turned his head and looked at her. She knelt beside him on the bed, barred with light from the rattan blind. Her dark hair was loose around her face, her dark eyes shadowed with worry. So young she broke his heart. He said, "You expect too much of yourself."

She covered his eyes with her free hand. "Sleep."

"You can only work with what we bring you. If we don't bring you the men who know ... who knew..." The darkness of her touch seeped through him.

"Sleep."

"Will you still be here?"

"Yes. Now sleep."

Three times told, he slept.

She had to be pure to work her craft, a virgin in the heart of army intelligence. He never knew if this loving would compromise her with her superiors. She swore it would not touch her power, and he did not ask her more. He just took her with his hands, his tongue, his skin, and if sometimes the forbidden depths of her had him aching with need, that only made the moment when she slid her mouth around him more potent, explosive as a shell bursting in the bore of a gun. And he laughed sometimes when she twisted against him, growling, her teeth sharp on his neck: virgin. He laughed—and forgot for a time the smell of long-dead men.

"Finest military intelligence in the world," Colonel Tibbit-Noyse said, "and we can't find their blasted army from one day to the next." His black moustache was crisp in the wilting heat of the briefing room.

Graham sat with half a dozen officers scribbling in notebooks balanced on their knees. Like the others, he let his pencil rest when the colonel began his familiar tirade.

"We know the führer's entrail-readers are prone to inaccuracy and internal strife. We know who his spies are and have been feeding them tripe for months." (There was a dutiful chuckle.) "We know the desert tribesmen who have been guiding his armoured divisions are weary almost to death with the Superior Man. For God's sake, our desert johnnies have been meeting them for tea among the dunes! So why the *hell*—" the colonel's hand slashed at a passing fly "—can't we find them before they drop their bloody shells into our bloody laps?"

Two captains and three lieutenants, all the company officers not in the field, tapped pencil ends on their notebooks and thumbed the sweat from their brows. Major Healy, sitting behind the map table, coughed into his hand. Graham, eyes fixed on the wall over the major's shoulder, heard again the rattle of gunfire, saw again the carnage shaded by vulture wings. His notebook slid through his fingers to the floor. The small sound in the colonel's silence made everyone jump. He bent to pick it up.

"Now, I have dared to suggest," Tibbit-Noyse continued, "that the fault may not lie with our intel at all, but rather with the use to which it has been put. This little notion of mine has not been greeted with enthusiasm." (Again, a dry chuckle from the men.) "In fact, I'm afraid the general got rather testy about the quantity and quality of fodder we've scavenged for his necromancer in recent weeks. Therefore—" The colonel sighed. His voice was subdued when he continued. "Therefore, all squads will henceforth make it their sole mission to find and retrieve enemy dead, be they abandoned or buried, with an urgent priority on those of officer rank. I'm afraid this will entail a fair bit of dodging about on the wrong side of the battle line, but you'll be delighted to know that the general has agreed to an increase in leave time between missions from two days to four." He looked at Graham. "Beginning immediately, captain, so you have another three days' rest coming to you."

"I'm fit to go tomorrow, sir," Graham said.

Tibbit-Noyse gave him a bleak smile. "Take your time, captain. There's plenty of death to go 'round."

There was another moment of silence, this one long enough for the men to start fidgeting. Healy coughed. Graham sketched the outlines of birds. Then the colonel went on with his briefing.

She had duties during the day, and in any event he could not spend all his leave in her company. He had learned from the nomads not to drink until he must. So he found a café not too near headquarters, one with an awning and a boy to whisk the flies, and drank small cups of syrupy coffee until his heart raced and sleep no longer tempted him.

A large body dropped into the seat opposite him. "Christ. How can you drink coffee in this heat?"

Graham blinked the other's face into focus: Montrose, a second-string journalist with beefy cheeks and a bloodhound's eyes. The boy brought the reporter a bottle of lemon squash, half of which he poured down his throat without seeming to swallow. "Whew!"

"We have orders," Graham said, his voice neutral, "not to speak with the press."

"Look at you, you bastard. Not even sweating." Montrose had a flat Australian accent and salt-rimmed patches of sweat underneath his arms. "Or have you just had the juice scared out of you?"

Graham gave a thin smile and brushed flies away from the rim of his cup.

"Listen." Montrose hunkered over the table. "There've been rumours of a major cock-up. Somebody let some secrets slip into the wrong ears. Somebody in intelligence. Somebody high up. Ring any bells?"

Graham covered a yawn. He didn't have to fake one. The coastal heat was a blanket that could smother even the caffeine. He drank the last swallow, leaving a sludge of sugar in the bottom of the cup, and flagged the boy.

"According to this rumour," Montrose said, undaunted, "at least one of the secrets had to do with the field manoeuvres of the Dead Squad—pardon me—the Special Desert Reconnaissance Group. Which, come to think of it, is your outfit, isn't it, Graham?" Montrose blinked with false concern. "Didn't have any trouble your last time out, did you, mate? No unpleasant surprises? No nasty Jerries hiding among the dunes?"

The boy came back, set a fresh coffee down by Graham's elbow, gave him a fleeting glance from thickly-lashed eyes. Graham dropped a couple of coins on the tray.

"How's your wife?" Graham said.

Montrose sighed and leaned back to finish his lemonade. "God knows. Jerries went and sank the mail ship, didn't they? She could be dead, and I'd never even know."

"You could be dead," Graham said, "and she would never know. Isn't that a bit more likely given your relative circumstances?"

Montrose grunted in morose agreement and whistled for the boy.

***

He stalled as long as he could, through the afternoon and into the cook-fire haze of dusk, and even so he waited nearly an hour. When she came home, limp and pale, she gave him a weary smile and unlocked her door. He knew better than to touch her before she'd had a chance to bathe. He followed her through the stuffy entrance hall to the airier gloom of her room. She stepped out of her shoes on her way into the bathroom. He heard water splat in the empty tub. Then she came back and began to take off her clothes.

He said, "I have three more days' leave."

She unbuttoned her blouse and peeled it off. "I heard." She tossed the blouse into a hamper by the bathroom door. "I'm glad."

He sat in a creaking wicker chair, set his cap on the floor. "There's a rumour going around about some misplaced intel."

She frowned slightly as she unfastened her skirt. "I haven't heard about that."

"I had it from a reporter. Not the most reliable source."

The skirt followed the blouse, then her slip, her brassiere, her underpants. Naked, she lifted her arms to take down her hair. Shadows defined her ribs, her taut belly, the divide of her loins. She walked over to drop hairpins into his hand.

"Who is supposed to have said what to whom?"

"There were no characters in the drama," he said. "But if it's true..."

"If it's true, then your men never had a chance."

This close she smelled of woman-sweat and death. His throat tightened. "They had no chance, regardless. Neither do the men in the field now. They've sent the whole damn company out chasing dead men." He dropped his head against the chair and closed his eyes. "This bloody war."

"It's probably just a rumour," she said, and he heard her move away. The rumble from the bathroom tap stopped. Water sloshed as she stepped into the tub. Graham rolled her hairpins against his palm.

Her scent faded with the last of the light.

He wished she had a name he could call her by. Like her intact hymen, her namelessness was meant to protect her from the forces she wrestled in her work, but it seemed a grievous thing. She was so specific a woman, so unique, so much herself; he knew so intimately her looks, her textures, her voice; he could even guess, sometimes, at her thoughts; and yet she was anonymous. The general's necromancer. The witch. The girl. His endearments came unravelled in the empty space where her name should be, so he took refuge in silence, wishing, as much for his sake as for hers, that she had not been born and raised to her grisly vocation. From childhood she had known nothing other than death.

"How can you bear it?" he asked her once.

"How can you?" A glance of mockery. "But maybe no-one told you. We all live with death."

He had a vision of himself dead and in her hands, and understood it for a strange desire. He did not put it into words, but he knew her intimacy with the dead, with death, went beyond this mere closeness of flesh. Skin slick with sweat-salt, speechless tongues and hands that sought the vulnerable centre of being, touch dangerous and tender and never allowed inside the heart, the womb. He pressed her in the darkness, strove against her as if they fought, as if one or both might be consumed in this act without hope of consummation. She clung to him, spilled over with the liquor of desire, and still he drank, his thirst for her unslaked, unslakeable until she, wet and limber as an eel, turned in his arms, turned to him, turned against him, and swallowed him into sleep.

The battle washed across the desert as freely as water unbounded by shores, the war's tidal wrack of ruined bodies, tanks, and planes left like flotsam upon the dunes. The ancient, polluted city lay between the sea and that other, drier beach, and no-one knew yet where the high tide line would be. Already the streets were full of the walking wounded.

Graham had errands to run. His desert boots needed mending, he had a new dress tunic to collect from the tailor—trivial chores that, performed against the backdrop of conflict, reminded him in their surreality of lying with two other soldiers under an overhang that was too small to shelter one, seeing men torn apart by machine gun fire, and feeling the sand grit between his molars, the tickle of some insect across his hand, and his sergeant's boot heel drum against his kidney as the man shook, as they all shook, wanting to live, wanting not to die as the others died, wanting not to be eaten as the others were eaten by the vultures that wheeled down from an empty sky and that could not be trusted to report the enemy's absence, as they were brave enough to face the living when there was a meal at stake. In the tailor's shop he met a man he knew slightly, a major in another branch of Intelligence, and they went to a hotel bar for beer.

The place looked cool, with white tile, potted palms, lazy ceiling fans, but the look was a lie. Strips of flypaper that hung inconspicuously behind the bar twisted under the weight of captured flies. The major paid for two pints and led the way to an unoccupied table.

"Look at them all," he said between quick swallows.

Graham grunted acknowledgement, though he did not look around. He had already seen the scattered crowd of civilians, European refugees nervous as starlings under a hawk's wings.

"Terrified Jerry's going to come along and send them all back where they came from." The major sounded as if he rather liked the idea.

The beer felt good going down.

"As I see it," said the major, "this haphazard retreat of ours is actually going to work in our favour before the end. Think of it. The more scattered our forces are, the more thinly Jerry has to spread his own line. Right now they may look like a scythe sweeping up from the south and west," the major drew an arc in a puddle of spilled beer, "but they have to extend their line at every advance in order to keep any stragglers of ours from simply sitting tight until we're at their backs. Any day now they're going to find themselves overextended, and all we have to do is make a quick nip through a weak spot"—he bisected the arc—"and we'll have them in two pieces, both of them surrounded."

"And how do we find the weak spot?"

"Oh, well," the major said complacently, "that's a job for heroes like you, not desk wallahs like me."

Graham got up to buy the next round. When he came back to the table, the major had been joined by another man in uniform, a captain also wearing the *I* insignia. Graham put the glasses down and sat, and only then noticed the looks on their faces.

"I say, old man," the major said. "Rumour has it your section chief has just topped himself in his office."

"It's not a rumour," the captain said. "Colonel Tibbit-Noyse shot himself. I saw his desk. It was covered in his brains." He reached for Graham's beer and thirstily emptied the glass.

Major Healy, the colonel's aide, was impossible to find. Graham tracked him all over headquarters, but, although his progress allowed him to hear the evolving story of the colonel's death, he never managed to meet up with Healy. Eventually he came to his senses and let himself into

Healy's cubbyhole of an office. The major kept a box of cigarettes on his desk. Graham seldom smoked, but, eaten by waiting, he lit one after another, the smoke dry and harsh as desert air flavoured with gunpowder. When Healy came in, not long before sundown, he shouted "Bloody hell!" and slammed the door hard enough to rattle the window in its frame.

Graham put out his dog end in the overcrowded ashtray. Healy dropped into his desk chair, and it tipped him back with a groan.

"Go away, captain. I can't tell you anything, and if you stay I might shoot you and save Jerry the bother."

"Why did he do it?"

Healy jumped up and slammed his fist on his desk. "Out!" The chair rolled back to bump the wall.

"He sent the whole company to die on that slaughterground, and then he killed himself?" Graham shook his head.

The major wiped his face with his palms and went to stand at the window. "God knows what's in a man's mind at a time like that."

"Rumour has it he was the one who spilled our movements to the enemy." Graham was hoarse from cigarettes and thirst. "Rumour has him doing it for money, for sex, for loyalty to the other side. Because of blackmail, or stupidity, or threats."

"Rumour."

"I don't believe it."

Healy turned from the window. The last brass bars of light streaked the dusty glass. "Don't you?"

"Whatever he'd done, I don't believe he would have killed himself before he knew what had happened to the men."

"Don't you?"

"No, sir."

"If he was a spy, he wouldn't give a ha'penny damn about the men."

"Do you believe that, sir?"

Healy coughed and went to the box on his desk for a cigarette. When he saw how few were left he gave Graham a sour look. He chose one, lit it with a silver lighter from his pocket, blew out the smoke in a long thin stream.

"It doesn't matter what I believe," he said quietly. "Now give me some peace, will you? I have work to do."

The sun was almost gone. Graham got up and fumbled for the door.

***

Blackout enveloped the city. Even the stars were dim behind the scrim of cooking smoke that hazed the local sky. Though he might have wheedled a car and driver out of the motor pool, he decided to walk. Her compound was nearly a mile of crooked streets away, and it took all his concentration to recognize the turns in the darkness. Nearly all. He felt a kinship with the other men of his company, men who groped their way through the wind-built maze of dunes and bony sandstone ridges, led by a chancy map into what could be, at every furtive step, a trap. He had seen how blood pooled on earth too dry to drink, how it dulled under a skin of dust even before the flies came. Native eyes watched from dim doorways, and he touched the sidearm on his belt. With the war on the city's threshold, everyone was nervous.

Her doorway was as dim as all the rest. In the weak light that escaped her room her eyes were only a liquid gleam. She said his name uncertainly, and only when he answered did she step back to let him in.

"I didn't think you'd come."

"I'm still on leave." A fatuous thing to say, but it was all he could think of.

She led him into her room where, hidden by blinds, oil lamps added to the heat. The bare space was stifling, as if crowded by the invisible. On her bed, the blue shawl she used as a coverlet showed the wrinkles where she had lain.

"It's past curfew," she said. "And..." She stood with her elbows cupped in her palms, barefoot, her yellow cotton dress catching the light behind it. Graham went to her, put his arms about her, leaned his face against her hair. She smelled of tea leaves and cloves.

"Of course you've heard," he said.

"Heard?"

"About the colonel. Tibbit-Noyse's suicide."

She drew in a staggered breath and pulled her arms from between them. "Yes." She returned his embrace, tipped her head to put her cheek against his.

He pulled her tighter. She was slight and strong with bone. Some pent emotion began to shake its way out of his body. As if to calm him, she kissed his neck, his mouth, her body alive against his. He could not discern whether she also shook or was only shaken by his tension. They stripped each other, clumsy, quick to reach the point of skin on skin. She began to kneel, but he caught her arms and lifted her to the bed.

He came closer than he ever had to ending it. Weighing her down, hard against the welling heat between her thighs, he wanted, he ached, he raged with some fury that was neither anger nor lust but some need, some absence without a name. Hard between her thighs. Hands tight against her face. Eyes on hers bright with oil flames. No, she said, and he was shaking again with the convulsive shudders of a fever, he'd seen malaria and thought this was some illness as well, some disease of heat and anguish and war, and she said "No!" and scratched his face.

He rolled onto his back and hardly had he moved but she was off the bed. Arms across his face, he heard her harsh breathing retreat across the room. The bathroom door slammed. Opened.

"Do you know about Tibbit-Noyse?"

Her voice shook. An answer to that uncertainty, at least.

"Know what?" he asked.

Her breathing was quieter, now.

"Know what?"

"That I have been ordered," she answered at last, "to resurrect him in the morning."

He did not move.

The bathroom door closed.

She had broken his skin. The small wound stung with sweat, or maybe it was tears, there beside his eye.

When she stayed in the bathroom, and stayed, and stayed, he finally understood. He rose and dressed, and walked out into the curfew darkness where, apparently, he belonged.

Next morning, Graham ran up the stairs to Healy's office and collided with the major outside his door.

"Graham!" Major Healy exclaimed. "What the devil are you doing here? Don't tell me. I'm already late." He pushed past and started down the hall.

Graham stretched to catch up. "I know. They're bringing the colonel back."

Healy strode another step, two, then stopped. Graham stopped as well, so the two of them stood eye to eye in the corridor. Men in uniform brushed by on their own affairs. Healy said in a furious undertone, "How the hell do you know about that?"

"I want to be there."

"Impossible." The major started to turn.

Graham grabbed his arm. "Morale's already dangerously low. How do you think the troops would react if they knew their superiors were bringing back their own dead?"

Healy's eyes widened. "Are you blackmailing your superior officer? You could be shot!"

"Sir. David. Please." Graham took his hand off the other's arm.

Healy seemed to wilt. "It's nothing you ever want to see, John. Will you believe me? It's nothing you ever want to see."

"Neither is all your men being shot dead and eaten by vultures while you lie there and do *nothing*. I owe them this!"

Healy shut his eyes. "I don't know. You may be right." He coughed and started for the stairs. "You may be right."

Taking that for permission, Graham followed him down.

The company's staging area was a weird patch of quiet amidst the scramble of other units that had to equip and sustain their troops in the field. Trucks, jeeps, men raced overladen on crumbling streets, spewing exhaust and profanity as they went. By the nature of their missions, reconnaissance squads were on their own once deployed, and this was never truer than for Special Recon. No-one wanted to involve themselves with the Dead Squad in the field. The nickname, Graham thought, was an irony no-one was likely to pronounce aloud today.

He and Major Healy had driven to the staging area alone, late, as Healy had mentioned, but when they arrived they found only one staff car parked outside the necromancer's workshop. The general in charge of Intel was inside the vehicle with two men from his staff. When Healy parked his jeep next to the car, the three men got out, leaving the general's driver to slouch smoking behind the wheel. They formed a group on the square of rutted tarmac that was hemmed in by prefabricated wooden walls, empty windows, and blinding tin roofs. The compound stank of petrol fumes, hot tar, and an inadequate latrine.

The general, a short bulky man in a uniform limp with sweat, returned Graham's and Healy's salutes without enthusiasm. He didn't remark on Graham's presence. Graham supposed that Healy, as Special

Recon's acting CO, was entitled to an aide.

The general checked his watch. "It's past time."

"Sorry, sir," Healy said. "We were detained at HQ."

The general grunted. He had cold pebble eyes in pouchy lids. "Any news of your men in the field?"

"No, sir. But I wouldn't expect to hear this early. None of the squads will have reached the line yet."

The general grunted again, and, though his face bore no expression, Graham realized he was reluctant to go in. His aides had the stiff faces and wide eyes of men about to go into battle. Healy looked tired and somewhat sick. Graham felt a twinge of adrenaline in his gut, his breath came a little short. The general gave a curt nod and headed for the necromancer's door.

Inside her workshop, the walls and the underside of the tin roof were clothed in woven reed mats. Even the windows were covered: the room was brilliantly and hotly lit by a klieg lamp in one corner. An electric fan whirred in another, stirring up a breeze that played among the mats, so that the long room was restless with motion, as if the pale brown mats were tent walls. This, the heat, the unmasked stink of decay, all recalled a dozen missions to Graham's mind. His gut clenched again and sweat sprang cool upon his skin. There was no sign of her, or of Tibbit-Noyse. An inner door stood slightly ajar.

The general cleared his throat once, and then again, as if he meant to call out, but he held his silence. Eventually the other door swung further open, and the girl put her head through.

Graham felt the shock when her eyes touched him. But she was in some distant place, her eyelids heavy, her face open and serene. He saw that she knew him, but by her response his was only one face among five.

She said, "I'm ready to begin."

The general nodded. "Proceed."

"You know I have lodged a protest with the Sisterhood?"

The general's face clenched like a fist. "Proceed."

She stepped out of sight, leaving the door open, and in a moment she wheeled a hospital gurney into the room, handling the awkward thing with practiced ease. Tibbit-Noyse's corpse lay on its back, naked to the lamp's white glare. The heavy calibre bullet had made a ruin of the left side of his face and head. A ragged hole gaped from the outer corner of his eye to behind his temple. The cheekbone, cracked askew, whitely defined the lower margin of the wound. The whole of his face was distorted, the left eye open wide and strangely discoloured, while the right eye showed only a white crescent. Shrinking lips parted to show teeth and a grey hint of tongue beneath the crisp moustache. The body was the colour of paste and, barring an old appendectomy scar, intact.

The hole in Tibbit-Noyse's skull was open onto darkness. Graham remembered the Intel captain saying the man's brains had been scattered across his desk. But death was nothing new to him, and he realized he was examining the corpse so he could avoid seeing the girl. Spurred by the realization, then, he had to look at her.

She wore a prosaic bathrobe of worn blue velvet, tightly belted at her waist. Her dark hair was pinned at the base of her neck. Her feet, on the stained cement floor, were bare. She set the brakes on the gurney's wheels with her toes, and then stood at the corpse's head, studying it, arms folded with her elbows cupped in her palms, mouth a little pursed.

An expression he knew, a face he knew so well. Another wave of sweat washed over him. He wished he had not come.

The fan stirred the walls. The lamp glared. Trucks on the street behind the compound intermittently roared past.

The girl—the witch—nodded to herself and went back into the other room but reappeared almost at once, naked, bearing a tray heavy with the tools of her craft. She set this down on the floor at her feet, selected a small, hooked knife, and then glanced at the men by the door.

"You might pray," she said softly. "It sometimes helps."

Helps the watchers, Graham understood her to mean. He knew she needed no help from them.

Her nakedness spurred a rush of heat in his body, helpless response to long conditioning, counter tide to the cold sweep of horror. Blood started to sing in his ears.

She took up her knife and began.

There is no kindness between the living and the dead.

Graham had sat through the orientation lecture, he knew the theory, at least the simplified version appropriate for the uninitiated. To lay the foundation for the false link between body and departed spirit the witch must claim the flesh. She must possess the dead clay, she must absorb it into her sphere of power, and so she must know it, know it utterly.

The ritual was autopsy. Was intercourse. Was feast.

Not literally, not quite. But her excavation of the corpse was intimate and brutal, a physical, sensual, savage act. As she explored Tibbit-Noyse's face, his hands, his genitals, his skin, Graham followed her on a tour of the lust they had known together, he and she, the loving that they had enacted in the privacy of her room and that was now laid bare. As the dead man's secret tissues were stripped naked, so was Graham exposed. He rode waves of disgust, of desire, of sheer scorching humiliation, as if she fucked another man on the street—only this was worse, unimaginably worse, steeped as it was in the liquors of rot.

He also only stood, his shoulder by Healy's, his back to the rough matted wall, and said nothing, did nothing, showed (he thought) nothing ... and watched.

When Tibbit-Noyse was open, when he was pierced and wired and riddled with her tools and charms, when there was no part of the man she had not seen and touched and claimed—when the fan stirred not air but a swampy vapour of shit and bile and decay—when she was slick with sweat and the clotting moistures of death—then she began the call.

She had a beautiful voice. Graham realized she had never sung for him, had not even hummed in the bath as she washed her hair. The men watching could see her throat swell as she drew in air, the muscles in her belly work as she sustained the long pure notes of the chant. The words were meaningless. The song was all.

When Tibbit-Noyse answered, it was with the voice of a child who weeps in the dark, alone.

The witch stepped back from the gurney, hands hanging at her sides, her face drawn with weariness but still serene.

"Ask," she said. "He will answer."

The general jerked his head, a marionette's parody of his usual brisk nod, and moved a step forward. He took a breath and then covered his mouth to catch a cough, the kind of cough that announces severe nausea. Carefully, he swallowed, and said, "Alfred Reginald Tibbit-Noyse. Do you hear me?"

A pause. "Y-ye-yes."

"Did you betray your country in a time of war?"

A pause. "Yes."

Graham could see the dead greyish lungs work inside the ribcage, the greyish tongue inside the mouth.

"How did you betray your country?"

A pause. "I sent my men." Pause. "To steal the dead." Pause. "Behind enemy lines."

The general sagged back on his heels. "That is a lie. Those men were sent out on my orders. How did you betray your country?"

A pause. "I sent my men." Pause. "To die." There was no emotion in the childish voice. It added calmly, "They were their mothers' sons."

"How did you know they were going to die?"

"...How could they." Pause. "Not be doomed."

"Did you send them into a trap?"

"...No."

"Did you betray their movements to the enemy?"

"...No."

"Then why did you kill yourself?" Against the dead man's calm, the general's frustration was strident.

"...I thought this war." Pause. "Would swallow us all." Pause. "I see now I was wrong."

Healy raised a hand to his eyes and whispered a curse. The general's shoulders bunched.

"Did you betray military secrets to the enemy?"

"...No."

"To whom did you betray military secrets?"

"...No-one."

"Don't you lie to me!" the general bellowed at the riddled corpse.

"He cannot lie," the witch told him. Her voice was quietly reproachful. "He is dead."

"...I do not lie."

The general, heeding neither the live woman nor the dead man, continued to rap out questions. Graham could bear no more. He brushed past Healy to slip through the door. In the clean hot light of noon he vomited spit and bile and sank down to sit with his back against the wall. After a minute, the general's driver climbed out of the staff car and offered him the last cigarette from a crumpled pack.

***

The battle became a part of history. The tide of the enemy's forces was turned before it swamped the city; a new frontline was drawn. The scattered squads of the Special Desert Reconnaissance Group returned in good time, missing no more men than most units who had fought in the desert sands and carrying their bounty of enemy dead. Graham was given a medal for bravery on a recommendation by the late Colonel Tibbit-Noyse, and a new command: twelve recruits from other units, men with stomachs already toughened by war. He led them out on a routine mission, by a stroke of luck found and recovered the withered husk of a major whose insignia promised useful intelligence, and on the morning of the scheduled resurrection, the second morning of his four-day leave, he went to the hotel bar where he had learned of Tibbit-Noyse's death and ordered a shot of whiskey and a beer.

He drank them, and several others like them, but the heat pressed the alcohol from his tissues before it could stupefy his mind. He gave up, paid his tab, and left. By this time the sunlight had thickened to the sticky amber of late afternoon. The ubiquitous flies made the only movement on the street. Graham settled his peaked cap on his head and blinked to accustom his eyes to the light, and when he looked again she was there.

She wore the yellow cotton dress. Her clean hair was soft about her face. Her eyes were wounded.

She said his name.

"Hello," he said after an awkward minute. "How are you?"

"My superiors have sent an official protest to the War Office."

"A protest?"

She looked down. "Because of the colonel's resurrection. It has made things ... a little more difficult than usual."

"I'm sorry to hear that."

"You have not—" She broke off, then raised her eyes to his. "You have not come to see me."

"I'm sorry." The alcohol seemed to be having a delayed effect on him now. The street teetered sluggishly beneath his feet. His throat closed on a bubble of air.

"It was hard," she said. "It was the hardest I've ever had to do."

Her dark eyes grew darker, and then there were tears on her face. "Please, John, I don't want to do this anymore. I don't think I can do this anymore. Please, help me; help me break free."

She reached for him, and he knew what she meant. He remembered their nights together, his body remembered to the roots of his hair the night he almost took her completely. He also remembered the scratch her nails had left by his eye, and, more than anything, he remembered her gruesome infidelity with Tibbit-Noyse—with all the other dead men—and he flinched away.

She froze, still reaching.

"I'm sorry," he said.

She drew her arms across herself, clasped her elbows in her palms. "I understand."

He opened his mouth, then realized he had nothing more to say. He touched his cap and walked away. The street was uneasy beneath his feet, the sun a furnace burn against his face, and he was blind with the image he carried with him: the look of relief that had flickered in the virgin's eyes.

J.R. CARPENTER

The Prettiest Teeth

Beth Wharton sits across the aisle from me. She has the prettiest teeth in the sixth grade. *My* teeth are a mess. One eyetooth is misshapen, and the other one never came in; one front tooth pokes through my lips if I smile, so I try not to. I try to keep my mouth shut altogether, but it's a losing battle. I can't stop myself. I crack lame joke after lame joke on the off chance that Beth Wharton will crack a smile.

Beth's teeth are as smooth and as perfectly even as my Grandmother Fisk's teeth—the ones she sets to soak in a pop-fizzy glass by her bedside every evening. I fished them out once when I thought no-one was looking. My mother was on me in an instant—she has eyes in the back of her head.

"You put those teeth down!" she hollered from the hallway.

I dropped them, missing the glass; they clattered onto the night table, chattering cartoon-style.

"You'll get those teeth eventually," my mother said. She wiped the dentures off on her T-shirt and plopped them back into the glass. "And don't blame me. You get your teeth from your father's side, not mine." I hadn't wanted my grandmother's dentures, not to keep. I only wanted, just for once, to run my tongue along a perfectly smooth set of teeth.

"Now who remembers: how do plants get their energy?"

Every time I raise my hand in class the other students squirm and groan. Mrs. Stalker should know better than to call on me.

"You water them with coffee?"

Not even funny, I know. I keep a straight face, of course, on account of my crooked front tooth. And I keep an eye on Beth Wharton. Sometimes she smiles, and sometimes she doesn't. I can never tell if a joke has really flopped or not until I've gone too far. One time, coming back from the bathroom, I forgot to close the classroom door behind me—Mrs. Stalker hates that.

"Alex Fisk! Were you born in a barn?"

"No. I was born in a hospital. They had swinging doors."

I got detention for a week that time. In detention Mrs. Stalker makes us write out dictionary pages longhand. So far I've copied up to F. Forsooth: in truth, often used to imply contempt or doubt. The sixth grade is almost over. I'm getting braces this summer. Forsooth, I can't wait for junior high.

On the last day of school the popular kids shake hands with the teachers and stand around the parking lot like big shots, talking like they're never going to see each other again. Everyone wants to leave but no-one wants to say goodbye.

It takes some doing to time it so Beth Wharton and I happen to walk out of the schoolyard together. We cross King Street. She turns off onto the Wentworth Road, and I keep pace. The sky is part racing bright and part low dark clouds. Beth is wearing last year's volleyball team T-shirt. I'm wearing an old spring jacket that I'm so sick of I consider flinging it into a passing hedge.

"How'd you do," she asks me part way up the hill. I have no idea what she's talking about. She has no bra on, and for once I'm not looking at her teeth.

"On your report card?" She waves her report card at me like I'm a total spaz.

"Oh. More of a greeting card, really," I say, faux-nonchalant.

"'Congratulations on your promotion!' And all that."

"Very funny," she grins, the tips of her teeth transparent in the sun. "Mine's more sympathy card. You know, like: 'Get well soon.'"

I laugh out loud. I can't believe it. Beth Wharton and I are actually almost sort of hanging out. "C'mon," I say. "Let's cut though the train tracks." It's not really a shortcut, just a different way around. We walk in jerky marionette-unison along the unevenly spaced railroad ties. Wind whips across the Fort Edward Mall parking lot, flinging grit at us. It's cold, for June.

"Here," I say, "want my jacket?" I drape my crappy windbreaker over Beth's shoulders. She accepts it with a shrug, or maybe she's just adjusting. I search along the side of the train tracks for something more to say. There are no raspberries yet, no loose spikes to pick up. The sun is at our backs. A low bank of dark cloud glowers in the sky ahead; a row of small white clouds stands out bright against them. Don't talk about the weather, I tell myself. For God's sake.

"Look," I say, "those little white clouds look like teeth."

"You don't have to try so hard, you know," she says.

"What?"

"I like you already. It's okay."

I stop in my tracks. On the tracks. "What did you say?"

"I bet your report card really says: "Alex Fisk has a smart mouth." She steps in front of me, her hair half apple juice golden, her face half in the shadow of my head.

"I bet your report card says—" my mind races through detention vocabulary. Formula: an established form or set of words.

"Stop talking." Beth Wharton reaches her arms up over my shoulders. My jacket slips off her back. I move my hands into the flesh-warm pocket of air at the small of her back. Our hipbones bump briefly. For the first time, I run my tongue along a set of smooth and perfectly even teeth.

Maya Stein

First Time

It was the first time I didn't want to have sex. With her, I mean. It was strange how it just happened like that, the way she stepped out of her clothes right in front of me, wiggled her ass the way she sometimes does to get my attention, then turned and glanced over her shoulder and gave me one of those looks that said, I'm here. A look that said, Please. And I don't know, was I doing something, reading or whatever, putting something away, was I doing something that begged for more attention, because whatever it was I didn't get up, didn't really stop what I was doing, didn't make a move even though she raised an eyebrow, as if to say *You coming?* because she was heading to the shower and we do that together a lot, shower, even for five minutes, even when we're in a hurry, and it felt a little strange not to want to follow her in, but I didn't, even with that look of hers I didn't follow her in, and she went in anyway, still wiggling her ass, she went in, and I realized that for the first time, the first time in a year and a half, I didn't want to have sex with her.

It was difficult even to look at her body, to see the flesh, to see it and not want to make love, to not want sex, to feel actually un-interested—in sex, in love, in her body—to watch her move away and feel a kind of relief. Her gone for a few moments and me not following her in. I didn't want to go, and I didn't want sex, and I didn't know what it meant, since she'd just moved in, a few weeks now, moved into my house and, fuck, it was like some big light switch being flipped, for the first time watching her undress and not wanting to make love, not even wanting to fuck, which is what I'd normally want to do in the middle of a weekend afternoon, and it was Saturday and four o'clock and I just didn't want to have sex, even if it was abundantly clear how much she wanted it, leaving the bathroom door open just in case I changed my mind, leaving a trail of her clothes leading out the door, jeans, her bra, her favourite black underwear, and I was hearing the shower going, hearing the pulse of it, and felt my own pulse quicken, because I just wanted to drop everything and run.

And what I really want to say is what it was like to look at her body the second before she left the room, look at her body with a kind of disgust, that's what I felt, disgust, the opposite of want, the opposite of love, I felt disgust, felt like I would never want to have sex with her again, worried that she'd come out of the shower wet and ready for a roll in the hay and it would be the last thing I could give her. If I stuck to my guts, my impulses, I'd get the fuck out of that room before she realized I was gone.

I wondered, wondered as I stayed right where I was, stayed and did the domestic thing, put away the laundry, straightened up, neatened up a bit, I wondered if anyone else I knew, any of my friends, ever looked at their lovers, their spouses, if they ever looked up in a similar innocuous moment like showers or bedtime, looked up and felt disgust too, saw the flaws, the unevenness, the close proximity of horror even, and if they willed the feeling away, if they squinted their eyes shut and gave the blowjob anyway, or let themselves be entered, if their kisses had a new bitterness to them, if they looked forward to sleep after it was all over, the sex over for the day, if they felt grateful for night falling, if they even faked it a little, yawned one of those fake yawns that are really just a way of expressing boredom, if they sacrificed that night's reading, the crossword, the moment they usually took for themselves, if they sacrificed that for the easy out of early sleep, shutting their eyes in regret, travelling away from where they were, the sheets, the smell of their lover, the wet spot their ass was inadvertently bumping into, if they wanted out like I did.

It was terrible really, the wanting out, the disgust, the seeing a body for its flaws, the not wanting to reach out and grasp, the retreat, the recoil, it was terrible. It was terrible how much I began to hate, sitting there and folding a small pile of T-shirts, how I began to hate her for her body, even, how I began to want a different body, just listening to the shower running and wanting to run to a different body, a harder body, a man body, a musk body, a body of sweat and six packs, God, I so wanted a body like that then, a body I could sink into, a body that would hold me, a firm, masculine, hard body, I wanted it, and I thought about the way her body was so unhard, unfirm, unmasculine and then felt like a year and half was an awfully long time to be having sex with a body I suddenly didn't want to have sex with anymore, and the guilt set in, so quick, the guilt set in, and I tried, I did, tried to change my mind, tried to conjure thoughts of the sex we'd had already, a year and a half in, the sex on the kitchen floor, the time I hung off the banister while she went down on me, the time on the outside deck, leaning against the railing with her fingers crawling inside, how I had to bite my lip to keep from screaming out, housemates down below twittering away their evening, how I held back, and how my body rocked in time to her hand, and then the time in the car, the first time, my hand on her breast, the front seat rolled back, her blouse undone, the windows steaming, and the time and the time and the time, and I thought about our recent Good Vibrations purchase, thought about how we came home that very afternoon and I strapped it on, how easy it was after the first fumblings, how easy it was to strap it on and enter her, how pleased I was, delighted I could do it, and amazed by how sexy it was to roll a condom on a dildo and feel like it was real, brought me back to the time I lost my virginity, the first time I saw a condom being rolled on a cock, it was sexy like that, and so I tried to think about this, about sex for the first time, about what it's like to be scared and exhilarated and naughty at the same time, how it feels to break the rules, stay out late, do something someone in your family might not approve of, do something outside of yourself like that.

And she came out of the shower somewhere in the middle of these thoughts, and, fuck, it's not easy to say this but it didn't work, the creative visualization didn't work, and I did the worst possible thing, I put down the laundry and looked at her as if to say *Yes*, as if to say *Come to me*, and she did, towel slipping off her waist, and revealing the body that I didn't want anymore, not today anyway, the towel slipped and something in me slipped too and I shrugged it off, tried to fight my way through it, saw that there would be no way to explain to her how much I didn't want this just now, but with the guilt, with the guilt I felt there was no choice, no choice but to rise up to her and reach for her hand, and then like a fucking liar pull her down to the bed, like a fucking liar I grabbed her ass, the ass she'd wiggled and the ass I'd looked away from five minutes ago, I grabbed it, grabbed it in a kind of earnest I guess, but what kind I don't know. It was almost anger, that much I can say, it was almost with a gesture of anger that I grabbed her, and it was indelicate. I grabbed her ass and then I grabbed onto her thighs and she let me, wanted it so badly, wanted so badly to be grabbed and clutched, and I guess that's what I did even though I was grabbing for some other thing, hope maybe, resurrection, a plea for it all to stop, the plummet from love and desire, I wanted it all to stop, I wanted to want her again, even just this once, I wanted it so badly I put all of that want into my hands, and then I put it into my mouth, and then the rest of my body, I pinned her to the bed, and it was so easy, she gave herself to me and I let myself have her, even in my deceit I let myself have her, and there was force to this sex, it became something less than sex, less than fucking, less than love, this is how I had her under my body, with something less than love. I took her like that, and it was not lovely, it was not the frolicky afternoon she wanted, it wasn't familiar to me at all, the way I took her, with fresh deceit and disgust. I felt ugly for this, and yet I was there, with my mouth holding her open, my palms pinning her thighs, there was violence in the room, and I wanted escape, from myself, from her, from the locking of our bodies, I wanted escape and this was the only way, to crawl with my mouth far inside of her, crawl for a kind of repentance. The feelings felt so ugly, and me, ugly too, I felt it, ugly for the way I was fucking her, because it was not lovely, it was not holy, it was not what I had ever intended, and after it was over she lay back so happy, felt ravaged, felt wanted, loved even, there was fresh love in her gaze, gratitude, and it felt like the worst kind of cruelty to me, to lie there like that with her, her hot neck resting on my arm, her chest expanding while my own heart, my own vicious little heart turned to stone.

IAN WATSON & ROBERTO QUAGLIA

The Penis of My Beloved

During my Beloved's lifetime his penis was of great importance to me—how could it be otherwise? Of course there was much more to my Beloved than his penis. For instance there was his tongue. I don't merely refer to his skill at licking, but also to all the words he said to me (except, obviously, while licking). Words are so important to a woman during love, just as they are in the everyday aspects of life. Also, there were his dark eyes, which spoke volumes of silent poetry. Also, there were his arms which held me. I need not enumerate more—there was all of Oliver. When my Beloved suddenly died of a heart attack, how desperately I craved to have him back again, alive.

This was possible due to advances in rapid cloning. However, a whole body cost a small fortune. Oliver and I had never given much thought to the morrow. Even by availing myself of a special offer from the Bodies'r'Us Clinic, and by paying on the instalment plan, the most I could afford was the cloning of a small part of Oliver.

Which part should it be? His right hand, sustained by an artificial blood supply and activated to a limited extent by a nerve impulse box with control buttons? Even a whole hand was out of my financial reach.

Should it be his tongue, likewise sustained by a costly blood supply?

Minus mouth and throat and vocal chords, a tongue could never say anything even if it wanted to, although it ought to be able to lick, for such is the nature of tongues. Body parts are aware of the role they play in the entirety of the body, consequently this memory lingers on even when they're amputated or dissected, or in this case cloned. Oh yes, his tongue ought to be able to lick, although the sensation might seem to me more like a warm slug than his robust tongue of yore.

How about one of his eyes, which spoke volumes? The eye could rest upon an eggcup and form an image of me. Before going to bed I could perform a striptease for his eye. Yet to be perfectly frank, what could his eye *do* for me? Also, although I had no intention of ever being unfaithful to my Beloved, a naked eyeball might seem like a spy camera keeping watch. This wasn't the kind of continuing intimacy I craved.

Really, my choice could only be the penis, especially as the cost was based upon the "normal" size when flaccid rather than erect. In this instance the money I would be paying in any event for the blood supply, so as to keep the part alive, would provide a special bonus benefit, namely erection when the penis was caressed. You couldn't say about any other cloned body part that your investment could grow ten-fold, as it were!

"You mightn't realize," the cloning salesman said to me, "that a penis becomes stiff not because of blood pumped actively into it by an excited body, but because certain penile muscles *relax*, which allows the blood to flow in and fill it. Normally the muscles are tense and inhibit the volume of blood—otherwise men would have permanent erections."

"So if you feel nervous and tense, you never get an erection?"

The salesman flushed, as though I had touched on a sore point. He was a young man with ginger hair and many freckles. The wallpaper of the consultation room was Klimt, so we were surrounded by hybrids of slender women and flowers.

"Madam, it's simply that you might be expecting too much. We can't absolutely guarantee erection, for that would be to alter the biology of the penis. In effect we would be providing you with a bio-dildo rather than with a genuine cloned organ—and we don't supply such things. Prostho-porn isn't our profession." This was spoken a shade tartly. The salesman may have been upset by my previous remark, supposing that it reflected upon his own virility.

I was sure that my Beloved's cloned penis would remember my own particular touch and wouldn't feel inhibited.

I made like a wide-eyed innocent. "Is 'prostho-porn' *anyone's* profession?"

"I've heard that in China..." The salesman lowered his voice. "Multiple cloned cunts of pop stars in pleasure parlours..." Now he seemed mollified and was all smiles again. "This won't be the case here! Your commission will be unique to you."

"I should hope so!"

It goes without saying that I'd arranged for sample cells from all of Oliver's important organs and limbs to be frozen in liquid nitrogen—

which wasn't too expensive—before the majority of his dear chilled body finally entered the furnace at the crematorium. I'd read that in another few years it might be possible to coax a finger or a penis, say, to diversify and regenerate from itself an entire body, but apparently this was a speculative line of research pursued by only a handful of maverick scientists. Small wonder: it's much more common for a body to lose a penis than for a penis to lose a body. So I was skeptical of this possibility. In the meantime my dream of recreating the entirety of Oliver, to rejoin his penis, would remain a dream because of the cost.

"So that's the famous penis!" exclaimed my neighbour Andorra, who was short and who spoke her own mind. Andorra and I were best friends even before the sudden death of my Beloved, about which she was very consoling. Currently Andorra was working for the Blood Donor Service.

Her parents chose the name Andorra for her, to suggest that she would be adorable. Naming her after the tiniest independent state in Europe did prove prophetic as regards her stature and personality—she was short and assertive. Yet as regards adorability in the eyes of the opposite sex, the ploy failed. Andorra had only ever had one boyfriend, and he was a disaster. No-one else tried to get into bed with her, or courted her. I think Andorra trained as a nurse due to reading too many doctor/nurse romance novels, many of which still littered her apartment, next door to mine.

Next door to *our* apartment, I should say. Oliver's and mine; mine and that of his penis.

Andorra's dog Coochie sometimes chewed her romance novels or carried them around her apartment while awaiting her return from work, and a walk, and an emptying. Coochie was a yellowish Labrador.

"Famous?" I replied. "There's nothing famous about it except in my own eyes." And in my hand, of course.

"It's a bit small..." but then she quickly added, "at the moment." She eyed the apparatus to which the penis was attached by two long connecting tubes. "Will you pump some more blood into it?"

So that she could behold an actual erect penis in the flesh at last?

"That isn't why a penis stiffens. Don't you know anatomy? What's important is the receptive mood of the penis."

"Well, it would be more impressive..." She tailed off.

Did she hope that I would stimulate the penis of my Beloved for her benefit? I almost succumbed to her implied entreaty, if only to demonstrate Oliver's penis in full gory, I mean glory, but this was an intimate matter.

"I'm perfectly satisfied," I told her. Only as I spoke did I realize how this might imply smugly that Andorra herself remained unsatisfied. She had mentioned dissatisfaction with dildos. I might seem to be cock-crowing, lording it over my friend.

Andorra looked thoughtful.

Due to the length of the blood tubes it was easy to take the penis to bed with me so as to stroke it in just the way my Beloved had liked, then pleasure myself after it stiffened. It remembered me. Because only Oliver's penis was cloned, not his prostate and other attachments, inevitably there was no ejaculation, yet this was no disadvantage—on the contrary! I would hold the rubber grip-mount, shaped like a small plantpot, in which his penis (as it were) grew, and much prolonged joy was mine. I was blissful. Sometimes after an orgasm I would take the penis out of me and talk to it, or use my mouth for a different purpose. I felt like a little girl: the penis of my Beloved, my lollipop.

But then came a problem with the blood supply—I don't mean the tubes and pump, but rather my finances. Bodies'r'Us strongly recommended renewing the blood each month to prevent degeneration of the penis. As part of the initial cost, I'd received five vouchers for replacement blood. Now I'd used those vouchers, and I discovered that in the meantime the cost of blood had risen by 25 percent.

Bodies'r'Us was a significant user and retailer of blood, needing to buy blood—good blood, too—from healthy sellers. Nobody would donate blood charitably so that some rich woman could maintain a clone of her dead poodle, or me a cloned penis. Andorra had complained to me that the Donor Service, which supplied hospitals, was suffering a bit of a blood drain because former donors were choosing to sell rather than donate, but luckily altruism and generosity still prevailed in society, not to mention donations by way of the vampire churches as part of their safe sex campaign.

At this point I consulted Andorra and she made me an offer...

...To smuggle blood from the Donor Service—providing that I let her use the penis of my Beloved privately one evening each week, say every Friday.

I was astonished and disconcerted.

"I'm your best friend," she pointed out.

"It won't respond to you," I said.

She pouted at me, full-lipped. "I'll find a way."

I should have refused. Yet if I refused, I might embitter Andorra. It must have cost her dear to make this request, this admission of craving for the real thing—or at least for the cloned and partial thing. Refusal might seem like a slap in the face. But also, of a sudden, I was curious as to whether my Beloved *would* respond to the touch of a stranger.

According to Andorra, the penis did react to her, and very satisfyingly, too. She might be fibbing so as to salve her pride, and I could hardly ask to be present while Andorra writhed on her bed. Besides, I wouldn't have wished to behold this personally. Consequently every Friday evening Andorra would carefully carry the pump and the penis along to her apartment and bring them back to me a couple of hours later. During this interval I would watch TV and try not to think about what might be happening. Once the penis was mine again, I would wash it, irrespective of whether Andorra had already done so. Washing excited the penis as much as caresses, since the actions were very similar. The penis seemed to be wishing to make up to me for what had occurred, even though it was I who owed the penis an apology.

I would kiss it. "Forgive me, my Beloved. You earned your blood, that's the main thing."

After some weeks I made a terrible discovery. When Andorra brought the penis back, Coochie was with her, pawing at her thigh and sniffing.

"Stay!" ordered Andorra, but Coochie pushed his way into my apartment. The dog's gaze was fixed on the now-floppy penis. He seemed to want it—not for a snack, which was my first fear, soon dispelled by a much worse realization: Coochie wanted the penis as a *penis*.

When I stared accusingly at Andorra, she broke down in tears of remorse.

"He's become addicted," she confessed.

"Do you mean ... do you mean ... you've been giving your dog *bestiality treats* with the penis of my Beloved?"

"He's an unusual dog! I love Coochie, and Coochie loves me, but I knew he was gay!"

"Gay? How did you know that?"

Andorra remained silent.

"Did Coochie bugger some other male dog while out walkies with you?"

More silence. My best friend couldn't tell me an outright lie. Suddenly I realized that if Andorra's discovery had *not* occurred during walkies then only one possibility remained...

"You used to try to get Coochie to fuck you! But no matter how you went about it, Coochie couldn't get it up because—"

"—Because Coochie's gay. It's the only explanation."

I felt sorry for Andorra. Yet I also had a persistent image in my mind ... of Coochie, who was gallumphing around, his anus frequently visible. How degrading for the penis of my Beloved!

While performing that canine service, Oliver's penis must have been stiff! Was the penis utterly undiscriminating?

"Look," I told Andorra, "you must promise me, don't do it with Coochie again. That's unhygienic."

"I always did me *after* I did Coochie."

That would have cleaned the penis?

Resulting in Andorra's vagina smelling of male dog? In due course Coochie might learn to associate ... Andorra had not given up hope.

"I'd be well within my rights to refuse you the penis ever again."

"And I to refuse you blood," she murmured.

She had a point. Consequently we didn't quarrel.

With some difficulty she hauled Coochie away. Alone once again, I eyed the wilted penis.

"Beloved, how could you do it with a dog?"

I tried to come to terms with what had happened by being objective and logical. The episode with Coochie was not my Beloved's fault.

The next week Andorra remarked, "Maybe the penis has erections in a Pavlovian way regardless of with whom or with what. Poor Oliver loves you, but he can't resist. You really ought to have more of him cloned."

How would I pay for that?

Oh, but she had the answer!

At the hospital where Andorra worked previously, she knew a junior anaesthetist who moonlighted as a stud in porn movies. Mark's rugged good looks and intelligence made him a desirable actor. As for his prowess, before each performance Mark would sniff a stimulant gas to keep himself stiff irrespective of ejaculation. Unfortunately Mark had recently been sacked for stealing gas from the hospital. Now he needed to rely full-time on porn to earn his living just at the time when he'd lost access to what boosted him.

What—suggested Andorra—if I were to offer the penis of my Beloved as a stand-in for Mark's penis while limp? With clever editing, viewers mightn't notice the temporary substitution, the tubes, the little plantpot clutched by Mark, or by whichever woman.

My Beloved's penis would be earning some money with which to recover more of himself for me.

"How is Coochie coping?" I asked.

"I lock him in the bathroom with a lot of cold turkey. He loves that. It takes his mind off the penis."

Andorra made arrangements. A couple of weeks later I watched a copy of the video in order to see with what sort of woman the penis was being unfaithful.

The poor editing hid little. It was obvious that part of the time a detached, hand-held penis was in use. Not a dildo, oh no, but a living penis which happened to lack a man attached to it.

What a dream for a woman, you may well say! And you would be right. Thanks to chat on the internet, word spread rapidly. The video became a wow among women. Few men bought it, maybe because of castration fears, but the producer was jubilant. Here at last was a porn video uniquely suited to females. Therefore we must make another video quickly—starring the detached living penis itself. Mark would play the role of a sex counsellor administering the penis as therapy to a patient. Not long after this second video was released, requests began arriving from dozens of sophisticated high society women requesting "private performances"—and offering to pay well.

Thus it was that at a private orgy, held in a woodland clearing on the outskirts of the city, the penis of my Beloved was mounted on the bonnet of a Jaguar car in place of the usual little model of a leaping jaguar. Several naked women wearing Venetian carnival masks took turns ascending the front of the car while friends cheered. This gave a new meaning to autoeroticism.

Because of those private performances I was accumulating money fast. A down-payment on cloning all the rest of my Beloved looked possible, not least because the wife of one of the directors of Bodies'r'Us was one of those who had privately enjoyed the penis of my Beloved. She regarded my quest for the entirety of my Beloved as so romantic.

This woman, Natalie, made short art films as a hobby. She was convinced that a film made by her about my eventual reunion with my Beloved might win her a prestigious award given for short art movies featuring sexual themes, the Shiny Palm. This trophy took the form of a feminine hand, in polished metal, grasping an erect penis made of purple glass.

On account of the porn movie about the autonomous penis, Bodies'r'Us had gained new customers. Wives who had seen that movie, and whose husbands failed to satisfy them sufficiently, urged their spouses to have their penises cloned so as to support the men's performance in bed. An identical understudy, or penis double, would increase the women's pleasure and offer extra possibilities.

Excellent publicity for Bodies'r'Us! In Natalie's opinion an artistic movie would add true chic to the cloning of small body parts.

Not necessarily always penises, either! A lovely nose might be cloned and mounted on a plaque, like a small hunting trophy, the blood supply out of sight in a hidden compartment. A hand might be cloned, or a finger. Due to lack of auxiliary muscles, one couldn't expect the hand to flex its fingers dramatically, or the finger to bend much. A finger is not a penis. Probably penises would be most popular.

"Rivalry might even arise among men who have cloned penises," Natalie declared to me on the phone one day. "Those can be displayed on the wall as a talking point at a dinner party. You know how men boast—but it would be most unsuitable for a man actually to pull his own trousers down during a fashionable dinner party! Besides, he mightn't rise to the occasion on account of too much alcohol or shyness. A cloned penis, which wouldn't imbibe, can represent him at his best. Wives will take pride in demonstrating the penis to their guests."

She speculated further: "Failure to mount your cloned penis on the wall might even give rise to suspicions as to the quality of the original penis. Too small? Too thin? Whatever! Maybe deficient men will buy more magnificent penises not cloned from themselves—provided by

Third World companies without the scruples of Bodies'r'Us. On the other hand, the display of a less-than-splendid penis on the dining room wall might be a form of inverted boastfulness: 'It may not look much, but if only you knew what I can do with it, and for how long!' You do want your Beloved back, don't you, dear? If you let me make a film about your quest, I'm sure Bodies'r'Us will be very easy on the terms for a full Beloved. My film wouldn't be intrusive, just a few remote-control mini-cameras concealed in your apartment."

I was so excited I would have agreed to almost anything.

Bodies'r'Us must have exploited some of that research by those maverick scientists I mentioned. Instead of cloning a 100 percent new body complete with brand new penis, they *integrated*—as they put it—the already-cloned penis into the ensemble of all the rest of Oliver's cloned anatomy. The cloned penis, which I already knew was precious to me—it stood for continuity. I could hardly discard it, but it would be downright silly to maintain that autonomous penis unused, expensively keeping a blood pump working at the same time as the full Oliver maintained a blood supply to another cloned penis by natural means. It was only sensible that the original cloned penis should be coupled to the rest of the clone.

And so my Beloved came back to me.

Along with some cameras and microphones for my apartment.

In years gone by, scientists predicted that a duplicated brain shouldn't retain any of the memories of the brain that it's cloned from. According to past scientific wisdom, the new brain would only exhibit the same capacities and personality traits and tendencies as the original brain—for instance the tendency to fall in love with somebody looking much like me, or the ability to learn languages easily.

Now we know that a cloned brain actually inherits many of the typical *dreams* of its source brain. This is because dreams are deeply archetypal. The original brain and the cloned brain are genetically identical, so by morphic resonance the cloned brain acquires much of the dream experience of the original from out of the collective storehouse from which dreams emerge and into which they return. Thus my cloned Beloved couldn't remember any actual incidents of our waking life together, but he knew who I was in a dreamy way. And because dreams contain speech, he could speak, although in rather a dreamlike manner.

"You are an almond tree," he told me, shortly after Bodies'r'Us delivered him to the apartment. Was that because of the colour of my eyes? If so, this must be an endearment.

Yet to my horror I very quickly found that my Beloved was impotent with me! No matter what I did, or how I displayed myself, his penis remained limp—that very penis which had previously responded so enthusiastically! This shocked and chagrined me—and I regretted the cameras and microphones Natalie had installed.

We have all heard how the arm of the executed German mass-murderer, Sigmund Hammerfest, was grafted on to an amputee, Rolf Heinz, who'd lost his arm in a car crash—and how the murderer's arm subsequently made Herr Heinz homicidal. While Herr Heinz was making love to his wife one night, the arm broke Frau Heinz's neck. The organs and limbs of the body possess a kind of memory, as I've said.

Could it be that, rejoined to its body, the penis conveyed memories of its multiple infidelities to my Beloved's body? And the body, now powering the penis, developed *guilt*, which disabled the penis? Thus the memory of the penis was contaminating the true wishes of its owner.

Yet what really *were* the true wishes of my Beloved? Could it be that the penis had truly loved me, but that Oliver himself as a complete person hadn't been quite so devoted? Could it be that formerly the penis had been ordering my Beloved to love me and nobody else? That it was the desire of the penis, rather than true love, which had made Oliver want to fuck me? Yet I had permitted the penis to respond to anybody; in a sense I had trained it to do so. Consequently now I was no longer a unique focus of desire. My Beloved might call me an almond tree like some medieval Arabian poet, but those were just pretty words! This was very confusing.

Why, oh why, had I cloned all of Oliver at such cost when the penis had been my real lover all along! I had prostituted the penis, the only part of him that truly loved me. Now Oliver was inhibiting the penis from performing, and I might be discovering all too late that my Beloved's flowery sentiments were hypocritical!

I accused my Beloved.

His replies were hard to understand—unlike the formerly clear, if nonverbal, responses of the stiff penis.

"You didn't truly love me," I cried.

"Balloons bring roses," said Oliver. "Scent escapes from bursting balloons." Did this mean that love dies?

"It was your penis that loved me, not you!"

"The rubies of your nipples are so hard they could cut glass." Was he complaining about my nipples? In the old days of our passion, had they hurt his chest?

I was shouting at him in angry disappointment when a knock came at the door.

Andorra stood outside, Coochie on a leash.

The blood froze in my veins. Here was the moment I had been fearing.

"May we come in?" Andorra asked with a big, insincere smile. The dog wagged his tail, excited, probably foreseeing who knows which kind of filthy development.

No, no, no! I thought with all the power of my mind. However, I heard my voice answer politely: "Yes, of course, feel at home." Oh, the hypocrisy of etiquette. I could have bitten off my tongue. But there was no escaping from destiny.

Oliver remained expressionless as he met the gaze of Andorra, then of the dog. Andorra was observing Oliver inquisitively, as if to perceive a penis improbably hidden between his eyes. The gay dog was salivating, detecting the smell of a friendly penis that it knew ... in the biblical sense. Coochie pushed close to Oliver and insolently sniffed his genitals through the trousers. Was the trace of an erection swelling in there? Oliver's forehead was knit. Did Coochie awake in him those dreams that I feared? Under no circumstances should I leave Oliver, and above all *my* penis, alone together with these two sexual jackals. As yet we were only in my hallway, which was quite large.

The doorbell rang again, and I turned to open the door once more. Etiquette!

Outside stood two mature women.

"We're from the Church for the Protection of Genital Organs," announced one of the ladies. "We'd like to interview you for our religious magazine."

This church had sprung up recently. Advances in plastic surgery were making it possible to have one's genitals exotically customized. Surely this insulted the sexual organs God designed for Adam and Eve

191

and for all of us! Biblical believers had long since abandoned defending the sanctity of marriage as a lost cause; consequently they poured their piety into defending the sanctity of copulation as God intended, using the exact organs He provided, not pudenda reshaped into orchids or trumpets, or giant clitorises or bifurcated dicks.

As I later discovered, Bodies'r'Us—who approved of exact copies, not baroque variations—had given some money to the Church of PGO and encouraged them to interview me to make an interesting scene in the movie. Drawing the attention of the Church of PGO was a big mistake, as subsequent events proved. But meanwhile I got rid of the two women as quickly as possible, although not fast enough. When I turned back to my guests, they were not there anymore. Andorra and Coochie had vanished along with my Beloved and his/my penis!

Obviously they had gone into the lounge, but why then had they closed the door? Worry clutched at me. I gripped the door handle to follow them only to discover that the door was locked! With a shiver I imagined the spectators of the movie seeing my face turn pale at this point as the most horrible of scenes formed in my mind, of my beloved Oliver buggering the Labrador, who in turn was buggering Andorra, who, between moans, was sipping champagne from one of the crystal glasses my grandmother had left me in her will.

Was the artistic, romantic movie of reunion with the Oliver of my penis destined to turn into the usual bestiality porn reality show, the commonplace of television? I banged loudly on the door, but the only response was what sounded like a suffocated whine. Nobody came to let me in to my own lounge.

"Oliver!" I shouted. "Andorra!" For answer, just another whine.

This was too much. I fainted.

When I recovered, I was lying on the couch in the lounge. Andorra and Oliver were watching me with worried expressions. Coochie was sitting, looking sleepy.

"How long have I been unconscious?"

"A few minutes," replied Andorra, whether this was true or not.

"We heard a thump and found you behind the door. You ought to have the handle seen to. I don't think it works properly."

Was she sincere?

"Why did you close the door at all?"

"To be discreet. You had visitors." Oh, etiquette again. If I believed her.

I turned to Oliver. "What happened in here before you found me passed out?"

"What is passed or past is the turd of the Fall, come Springtime."

In other words, *No use crying over spilt milk?* By which he might mean spilled semen. Did *turd* allude to a dog's anus? To my mind those two items are always closely linked. Oliver was no help at all. I'd been getting along better with his, or rather *my* penis.

Ignoring the gaze of my Beloved, I looked lower, so as to distinguish within his pants my more beloved penis, probably the only part of Oliver which ever really loved me. That wasn't difficult—an evident protuberance seemed likely to perforate his pants at any moment. Obviously Oliver's penis was completely erect, the way I remembered it, the way I had long loved it. Hidden as it was by trousers, I couldn't actually see it, and this seemed unjust. Forgetting about the presence of Andorra and the hidden cameras, instinctively I reached out a hand sweetly to caress my beloved penis, which I hadn't seen—nor felt—in its full, majestic, generous erection for far too long. In the very moment when my hand grazed it, the penis imploded like a Hindenburg airship, deflating at once and evading my contact. Suddenly everything became atrociously clear beyond any doubt!

The penis itself could not know so quickly that it was me who touched it, because the trousers were a barrier to its sensitive nerve endings. Therefore the order to deflate must have come directly from the brain of Oliver. I became furious and shouted: "You treacherous fuckface prickhead, get out of my home! Get out, but leave my penis here!"

Seizing Oliver, I propelled him with all my strength out of the lounge, through the hall, to the front door. He didn't resist but let himself be thrown out, although of course he took my/his penis with him. Those two damn churchwomen were still loitering outside, index fingers scribbling on smartscreens nestling in their palms. Were they inventing a nonexistent interview? Aurora and Coochie hurried past me without a word or a woof, and I slammed the door behind them. Then I allowed myself the wisest feminine recourse in emergency circumstances: I began to cry.

***

Oliver took up residence in Andorra's flat. Some days later a man with the face of a mummified pig presented himself at my door.

"I'm the lawyer of the penis," he introduced himself.

I discovered that the Church for the Protection of Genital Organs had arrogated to itself the right to represent the interests of Oliver's penis. From Pigface I heard talk about the rights of genital organs to self-determination and about some Treaty of Independence from the Bearer of the Organ. Oh the mysteries of jurisprudence! The ways that lawyers get rich!

Pigface explained to me that Oliver's penis had gained the status of an individual by virtue of having lived independently for a sufficient time before finding itself again attached to a human bearer. The Church for the Protection of Genital Organs was entitled to represent the penis because it was the first to claim that right, without the penis raising any objection.

"But the penis wouldn't be able to understand any of this!"

"Exactly. So it needed legal representation."

Later I learned how the judge at the court in question had become obsessed with making controversial landmark judgements in the hope of being retired soon with a knighthood or some other honour. The Church of PGO had been well aware of this.

In Andorra's flat there were no hidden cameras. Andorra had refused the TV company permission to install any cameras in her home— probably so as not to expose to the world her affair with the dog. For the TV company and for Bodies'r'Us this was unacceptable. On the other hand, the impotence Oliver's penis displayed toward me when it was attached to Oliver hardly made his return to my own home a very exciting prospect for Natalie and the other people involved in the production of the movie. The public doesn't much care for erotic dramas with impotent characters. Therefore the lawyers for Natalie and Bodies'r'Us were petitioning to have Oliver and his penis separated again, so that the penis could go back to performing in the role that had made it so famous: the penis without a man.

The penis without its Oliver had already become a star. A poll revealed that as an anonymous part of a normal person it wouldn't be so interesting to people.

The Church for the Protection of Genital Organs likewise wanted the penis to be separated from Oliver, yet not so that it could perform in porn movies or couple with me again, which they viewed as unnatural. Instead, they wanted it to retire to a Zen monastery. Oh, the moral obsessions of churches!

Thus there was conflict between the movie producers, with whom I had signed an agreement on behalf of the cloned Oliver, and the lawyers for the penis and the Church of PGO.

"We won't allow you to go on sexually exploiting that poor penis," Pigface told me at a deposition hearing.

"It's a sexual organ. It was born to be sexually exploited," I retorted.

"He's an individual with full rights, included the right of freely choosing the modality of his sexuality."

"It's a penis. If it becomes hard, that means it wants to fuck."

"Not at all! Diseases exist, such as priapism. Erection can be the symptom of a pathology."

I decided to change my strategy.

"It's a piece of meat without a brain. It's not compos mentis."

"Another reason to protect his dignity. We will never allow that poor penis to be forced into any more intercourses for which he didn't give written consent."

"How can a penis write anything?"

"If held properly, it can produce a DNA signature."

"Without a prostate it can't ejaculate, so where's the ink?"

"We can prepare all necessary documents *before* the separation."

Suits and countersuits were heard, and the lawyers were all very happy until at last no legal problems prohibited the penis being separated from Oliver. Final judgement was that since the penis was cloned *before* the body, *it* was the one who owned the other, and not the contrary. The penis owned the man, namely the cloned Oliver; Oliver did not own the penis. If it's legitimate for a man to cut off his own penis, provided that he isn't attempting suicide, logically the penis could decide to cut off its own man. The lawyer for the penis, as his legal representative, had full power to act in this regard—and to *steal* the penis of my Beloved, I was thinking in anger and frustration.

The judge duly retired and became a Lord.

***

However, we live in a strange and unpredictable world.

Under its various Patriot Acts, the USA had permitted itself to intervene in any part of the world in defense of its homeland security and its supplies of oil and cheap obesity fast food full of oil and sugar and additives. To signal to the world its rise as a rival superpower, China enacted the Salvation of Culture Law, by which the Chinese gave themselves the right to intervene anywhere to protect the interests of art. This was something that the American government found hard to understand, so they did not threaten the Chinese with thermonuclear war.

If the USA was the Global Cop, China would be the Global Curator. A popular US slogan was *Kick Ass America!* So Beijing declared *Save Art China!*—and why not, China being the oldest civilization on Earth? When Venice began to sink rapidly, swift intervention by Chinese technology had rescued the Italian city, preserving it in a dome to the applause of most nations. From then on, China could take great liberties in the defense of art.

Art included performance art, and one of the many ways of preserving art was Gor-Gon, a polymerizing nanotechnology inspired by Gunther Von Hagen's corpse plastination factory in the northeastern Chinese port city of Dalian. In just a few seconds, a jab of Gor-Gon administered by injection or by a dart fired from a gun could transform any living being into plastinated artwork, petrifying forever (though by no means as stiffly as stone) the target animal or person at that moment.

The penis had been quite a performer; and the legal case was by now notorious worldwide, as was the prospect of cloned penis and cloned person parting company. So Chinese art agents targeted Oliver. Already Chinese art agents had overenthusiastically targeted several famous opera singers and actors for a Hall of Fame. Since the salvation of Venice the Chinese could do pretty much as they pleased, but plastinating artists suddenly while they were on stage caused demands for ticket refunds, arguments about civil rights, and also poorer performances by many divas and stars who didn't wish to be plastinated; which was all very regrettable and counterproductive. So this was made illegal. But according to Chinese law plastinating a clone was just as acceptable as plastinating a criminal for export to medical schools...

***

I'm so lucky. At the moment of petrification, the penis of my former Beloved was fully erect—he had to be slid out of Andorra by the Chinese agents who invaded her flat. So now I live in China, inside a big transparent cube. I couple with the penis attached to Oliver whenever I want. Plastination keeps the penis stiff, yet soft and comfortable to use. Of course plastinated Oliver never says a thing, nor moves, although I arrange him artistically just as I please.

Outside the cube every day crowds of visiting art lovers and connoisseurs admire us and shoot holographic movies, so that we never feel alone. Inside the cube, the air is always fresh and rich in happy-making hormones. The Chinese takeaway meals supplied to me free are so varied and delicious. Life is beautiful! Or maybe life is simply too complex to understand.

About the Authors

Matthew Anderson is a parish pastor and lecturer in New Testament at Concordia University's Department of Theology, Montreal. His work has appeared in two other Véhicule Press anthologies, as well as on CBC Radio One and in *Maisonneuve* and *Grain*.

Ashok Banker's dark fiction has appeared in *Weird Tales, Gothic.Net, Altair, Artemis, Interzone, Utopiales Nantes*, and *Best New Fantasy 2*, has been translated into German, French, Hebrew, and several other languages, and was nominated for a Bram Stoker Award. He lives in Mumbai, India.

J.R. Carpenter is a poet, fiction writer, and new-media artist, originally from rural Nova Scotia, now living in Montreal. Her short story "Precipice" won the 2003-2004 CBC/QWF Short Story Competition and appeared in the anthology *Short Stuff: New English Stories from Québec*. Her poems and short stories have also appeared in *Carte Blanche, Carve, Nth Position, Knight Literary Journal*, and *Blood & Aphorisms*. Her web art projects have been exhibited internationally and can be found online at Luckysoap.com.

Robin Evans's stories can be found in *Outercast, Pindeldyboz, Thieves Jargon, Ken*Again*, and *Skive*, among others. She's contributed nonfiction to the anthology *Get on the Bus*, produced by San Francisco's CitySpace. If the writing doesn't do it first, Robin has a husband, a teenage daughter, and a small dog who promise to drive her crazy. She lives in Vancouver.

Tess Fragoulis was born in Heraklion, Crete, and grew up in Montreal, where she currently lives and writes. Her first book, *Stories to Hide from Your Mother* (Arsenal Pulp, 1997), was nominated for the QSPELL First Book Award in 1998. Her novel *Ariadne's Dream* (Thistledown Press) was longlisted for the IMPAC Dublin Literary Prize. She has recently completed a second novel, *The Goodtime Girl*, set in 1920s Greece and Asia Minor. She teaches fiction at Concordia University.

Harold Hoefle has published short fiction in Canadian anthologies and journals, including *Exile* and *Grain*. In 2003, Black Bile Press released his four-story chapbook *Spray Job*. "Waiting for My Father," a personal essay, appeared in *Maisonneuve* in 2005. Born in Toronto, Harold now teaches and writes in Montreal.

Nairne Holtz is a Montreal-based writer. Her short fiction has appeared in numerous literary journals and anthologies. She's currently editing an anthology of Canadian lesbian literary fiction. She has also created an annotated bibliography of Canadian literature with lesbian content (www.canadianlesbianliterature.ca).

Nalo Hopkinson (www.sff.net/people/nalo/), winner of the World Fantasy Award and Canada's Sunburst Award for her collection *Skin Folk*, is the author of the novels *Brown Girl in the Ring*, *Midnight Robber*, and *The Salt Roads*. She grew up in the tropics and now lives in Toronto.

Joel Hynes is the author of the novels *Down to the Dirt*, which won the Percy Janes First Novel Award and was nominated for the Dublin IMPAC Literary Award, and *Right Away Monday*, due for release in 2006. He is an award-winning playwright and actor. He's currently a series regular and contributing writer for the CBC's *Hatching, Matching and Dispatching*. His second novel, Hynes lives in St. John's, Newfoundland. "Lost Cause" is an excerpt from a work in progress, "Say Nothing Saw Wood."

Neil Kroetsch is a writer, actor, and translator living in Montreal.

Catherine Lundoff is a professional computer geek and transplanted Brooklynite who lives in Minneapolis with her fabulous partner. Her short stories have appeared in such anthologies as *Stirring Up a Storm*, *Naughty Spanking Stories from A to Z*, *Hot Women's Erotica*, *Blood Surrender*, *Ultimate Lesbian Erotica 2006*, *The Mammoth Book of Best New Erotica 4*, and *Best Lesbian Erotica 2006*. Torquere Press released a collection of her lesbian erotica, *Night's Kiss* (2005), and she pens the bimonthly writing column "Nuts and Bolts" for the Erotica Readers & Writers Association (www.erotica-readers.com).

Mark Paterson (markpaterson.ca) was born in San Francisco and grew up in Montreal, where he lives and writes. His first book, the short-story collection *Other People's Showers*, was published by Exile Editions. Mark was the co-host of the late and lamented cabaret series Grimy Windows Variety Showcase.

Holly Phillips has lived in British Columbia for most of her life, with some time out for work, education, and travel. Her debut story collection, *In the Palace of Repose*, has received wide critical praise, and her first novel, *The Burning Girl*, is a 2006 release from Prime Books. A full-time writer and editor, Holly shares her funky little house with several dozen refugee ladybugs and her cat, Savoy.

Scott D. Pomfret (www.scottpomfret.com) is co-author of *Hot Sauce* (Warner Books, 2005), one of the Romentics-brand romance novels for gay men (www.romentics.com). Pomfret's short stories have been published in *Post Road*, *Genre Magazine*, *Fresh Men: New Gay Voices*, *Best Gay Love Stories 2005* and *2006*, *Best Gay Erotica 2005*, and many other magazines and anthologies. He was born in Wellesley, Massachusetts, and now lives in Boston.

Roberto Quaglia (www.robertoquaglia.com) is an Italian surrealist author. With Ian Watson, he's collaborating on a series of "My Beloved" stories, which will become a book in due course. Other stories in the series are scheduled to appear in the anthology *Strange Pleasures* and the fantasy magazine *Weird Tales*.

Dan Rafter is a freelance writer living in Chesterton, Indiana. He usually writes about subjects far less interesting, for publications that are far less erotic.

Neil Smith has published in the anthology *Coming Attractions 04* (Oberon Press) and in volumes 14, 16, and 17 of *The Journey Prize Stories* (McClelland & Stewart). In early 2007, Knopf Canada will release his first book, *Bang Crunch*, as part of its New Face of Fiction program. Neil lives in Montreal.

Maya Stein is a writer and editor living in San Francisco. She's self-published two collections of erotic-themed essays, *The Overture of an Apple* (2003) and *Spinning the Bottle* (2002), and keeps a twice-weekly poetry blog at www.papayamaya.blogspot.com.

Ray Vukcevich (www.sff.net/people/RayV/) is the author of the collection *Meet Me in the Moon Room* and the novel *The Man of Maybe Half-a-Dozen Faces.* He lives in Oregon.

Ian Watson (www.ianwatson.info) is an award-winning British speculative-fiction writer and the author of some forty novels and collections. He wrote the screen story for Steven Spielberg's *A.I.* His satiric erotic novel *Orgasmachine* was a bestseller in Japan.

Barry Webster's writing has appeared in *Event, Fiddlehead, Matrix, Prairie Fire, Lichen,* and *Short Stuff: New English Stories from Québec.* His first collection of short stories, *The Sound of All Flesh,* was released by Porcupine's Quill Press in 2005.

Vic Winter (www.stemsandfeathers.org/vwinter) was born in Halifax, raised in Montreal, and currently lives in Ottawa; perhaps it is no surprise that Vic loves winter best of all the seasons. Vic stays warm on cold winter nights writing erotica. Words and snow, silence and long nights, the fall of rain and of silk, and love are some of Vic's other favourite things.

About the Editors

Claude Lalumière (lostpages.net) has edited five previous anthologies exploring various themes and genres, including *Island Dreams: Montreal Writers of the Fantastic* and, in collaboration with Marty Halpern, *Witpunk*. He's a prolific critic and short-fiction writer. His work has been anthologized in *The Best of SDO*, *Tesseracts 9*, *The Book of More Flesh*, *Mythspring: Stories Inspired by the Lyrics and Legends of Canada*, and the fourth and fifth volumes of *The Mammoth Book of Best New Erotica*. He blogs at lostpagesfoundpages.blogspot.com.

Elise Moser's fiction has appeared in *Prairie Fire*, *Descant*, *Broken Pencil*, and several anthologies. She won the 2003-2004 CBC/QWF Short Story Competition and earned an Honourable Mention in 2004-2005; her story "Or Be Killed" was Highly Commended in the 2005 Commonwealth Short Story Competition. Her poetry has been featured in the webzines *Carte Blanche* and *Nth Position*. She lives in Montreal.